ENCHIRIDION
OF POPE LEO

ENCHIRIDION LEONIS PAPÆ

SERENISSIMO IMPERATORI CAROLO MAGNO

IN MUNUS PRETIOSUM DATUM NUPERRIME MENDIS OMNIBUS PURGATUM

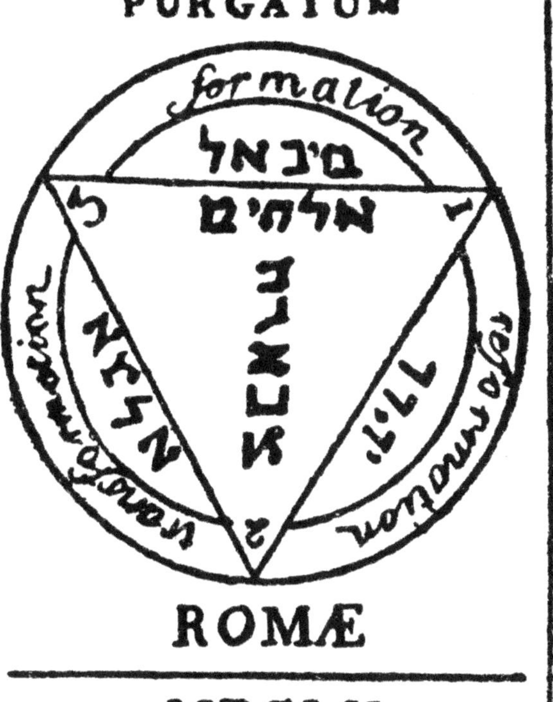

ROMÆ

MDCLX

TO THE WISE
CABALISTS

*I*T *is only after painstaking and assiduous research that we have succeeded in perfecting and complete The Enchiridion of Pope Leo. All the different editions of this work, of which we are in our possession, from Parma, Mainz, Ancona, Rome, Lyon and Frankfurt, etc., have enabled us to present it to the Curious with more order and accuracy than it has hitherto appeared. The way to use it varies in almost every edition of this Work, and it is perhaps because of these various changes, or because one finds some analogy with the Author's name, that it has been nicknamed the Butterfly. One finds in the various impressions of this Book of the Seven Psalms we have omitted, adding instead the virtues of these same Psalms, with the Character and name of the spirit to* *which they refer, from the Cabala. Charlemagne, to whom this work is dedicated as a token and precious treasure, was the first to know, through experience, their surprising and marvellous effects; he recited the Orisons with veneration, his face turned to the rising Sun, and vowed to carry them on his person, written in gold lettering: all the figures with which the Book is decorated are taken from the rarest manuscripts handed down to us, and they are adherent to the Orisons where they are found; they operate by carrying them. One can consult, about them, the Magical Calendar of the Occult Philosophy by the famous Agrippa.*

IN
VINCE
HOC

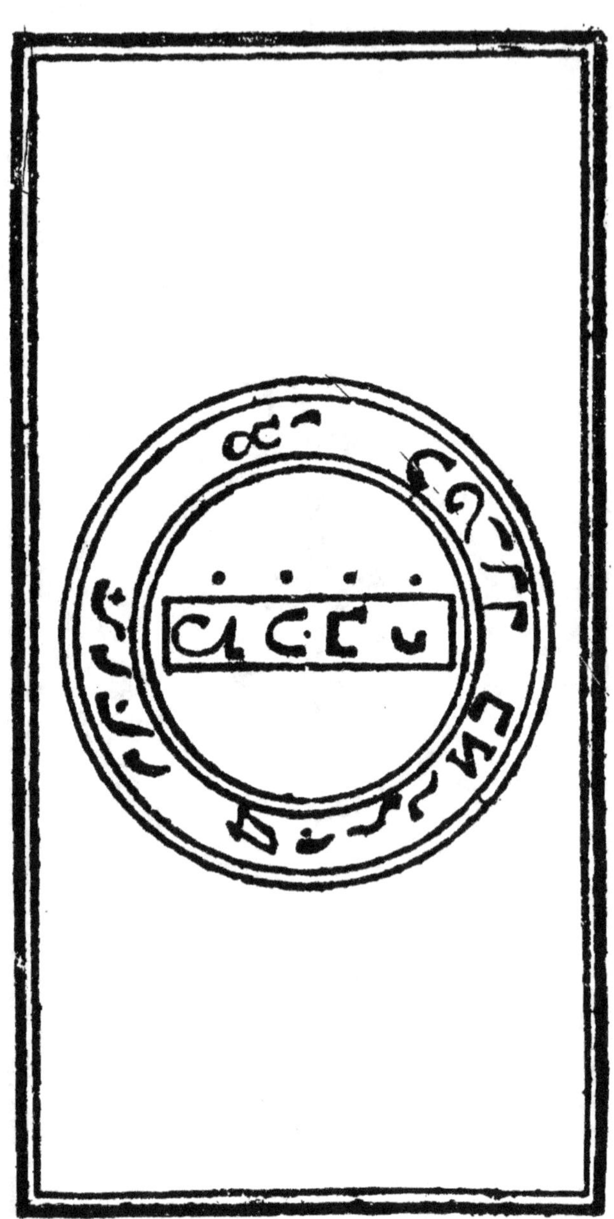

IN the beginning was the Word, and the Word was with God, and the Word was God. He was in the beginning with God. All things were made through him, and without him was not anything made that was made. In him was life, and the life (of Grace) was the light of men. The light shines in the darkness, and the darkness has not overcome it. There was a man sent from God, whose name was John. He came as a witness, to bear witness about the light, that all might believe through him. He was not the light, but came to bear witness about the light. The true light, which gives light to everyone, was coming into the world. He was in the world, and the world was made through him, yet the world did not know him. He came to his own, and his own people did not receive him. But to all who did receive him, who believed in his name, he gave the right to become children of God, who were born, not of blood nor of the will of the flesh nor of the will of man, but of God (being regenerated by the Sacrament, and the Grace of Jesus Christ). And the Word became flesh and dwelt among us, and we have seen his glory, glory as of the only Son from the Father, full of grace and truth. Let us give thanks to God.

Psalm 6. *Domine, ne in furore tuo arguas me, etc.*

DAVID wrote this Psalm to ask God for victory over his son, Absalom, and forgiveness for his sins. If said devoutly, it comforts the sinner and removes sadness for having offended God, and it converts him into joy and love.

Saint Cassiadore says that those who say this Psalm three times devoutly will change the unwillingness of an iniquitous Judge, and hinders being condemned wrongfully.

It is good against all work and torments of the mind, saying it seven times when in need, naming each time, the name of its Intelligence, then saying: *"I pray to thee ISU, Lord of salvation, by the virtue of thou Holy Names and of this Psalm, that thou deliver me from N. torments or evil from which thou can deliver as thou please."*

It is good against eyes sickness, if one says it seven times a day for three days in a row, and naming at the end its Intelligence, and each time write its Character on a Lettuce leaf of which one must touch the eye. The name of the Intelligence is HAEL, and this is his Character. (Fig.1 p.36.)

PSALM 31. *Beati quorum remissæ
sunt, etc.*

IT is used to know if God has forgiven our sins, and against the bites of dogs and snakes, and particularly the verse *in chamo et freno, etc...* It is also good for those who have hidden crimes and fear to be discovered, if they say it three times, every day, with the name of the Intelligence, which is necessary to write on the chest with its Character, and one will never speak about it. The name of the Intelligence is HUNEL, and this is his Character. (Fig.2)

PSALM 37. *Domine, ne in furore
tuo arguas me, etc.*

SAINT Jerome and Saint Augustine ensure that he who says it devoutly obtains the remission of his sins, and exempts him from the punishment he deserves. It cures epilepsy[1], if one writes it on a silver blade with a punch, when Mars is in good aspect with the Moon, with the name and Character of the Intelligence, on Tuesday and its Intelligence and Character, and have the patient say it for seven straight days in the morning and evening, and have him wear the said blade around his neck. The name of the Intelligence is RAMIACH, and this is his Character. (Fig.3)

PSALM 50. *Miserere mei, Deus, secundum magnam, etc.*

DAVID having taken Bathsheba after the death of Uriah, her husband, and the Prophet Nathan having taken her back, as we see in the second book of Kings, chapter 12, then knowing her sin, made this Psalm

---

1   *Mal caduc.* Ed.

which has the virtue of giving contrition; he composed it by the command of God. Saint Jerome says that it makes us obtain the remission of our sins, if we say it every day since they were committed. Saint Augustine assures that they will be forgiven, and that we will go to Heaven, which makes it admirable. Saint Ambrose calls it the glorious Psalm, and useful for the health of the body and soul, saying it every day, and against temptations, if we say it three times a day with its Intelligence on linen oil, and with this oil one marks the Character over the heart region. The name of the Intelligence is JENDSEL, and this is his Character. (Fig.4)

PSALM 101. *Domine, exaudi orationem meam, etc.*

DAVID made this Psalm because of the people of Israel who were to be delivered by the coming of Jesus Christ, as it is written in the second book of the Maccabees. This Psalm must be the seventh of the Penitential, with good reason. Saint Jerome assures that whoever says it devoutly every day will be wonderfully comforted in all his afflictions. To make conceive a woman who cannot have children, it is necessary to write with devotion on white taffeta the Intelligence and Character below, with the blood of a Dove, and the woman must carry it always, hung around the neck, and when she lies with her husband, let her not fail to turn it behind her back, between the shoulders, so that it hangs along the spine. The name of the Intelligence is SILTI or SILLI, and this is his Character. (Fig.5)

PSALM 125. *De profundis clamavi
ad te, Domine, etc.*[2]

THIS Psalm was sung in the second degree, representing that the Church of God prays incessantly for sinners; in order to erase the stains of their crimes. Saint Jerome says that David was converted by its virtue, as was the apostle Saint Paul, and the people of God delivered. Saint Augustine calls this Orison truly penitential, because it is very useful for the dead among all other gradual Psalms. It is good against storms and temptations, and the same Saint says that this prayer has always been answered by God, when it was said devoutly. It serves to have revelation in a dream, if one writes its Intelligence and its Character on three Cedar leaves, putting them under the head on the beside of the

---

2   Actually, *De profundis clamavi...* corresponds to Psalm 129 Vulgate. Ed.

bed when entering there, and saying three times the Psalm, and three times: *"I pray thee Hassard, that this night thou clearly show me the answer to the thing I wish to know."* The name of the Intelligence is STILU, and this is his Character. (Fig.6)

PSALM 142. *Domine, exaudi orationem meam, etc.*

To serve as an instruction, God told David that he would never be delivered from his enemies and enter his kingdom, had he not made this Psalm, which is called the Weeping Orison of David, by whose virtue he had all that he asked; because the Holy Spirit guided him in all his actions. Its virtue leads us by the spirit of God to all glorious places filled with spiritual and temporal goods. Saint Jerome says that it provides salvation of the body and soul of all the other

Psalms. It is penitential and of great virtue. It is good for travellers by sea and land, and for those who seek offices and dignities; if they are good people, the Holy Spirit will teach them the way they should look, and will keep them on the days that they have said it. Saint Jerome claims to have experienced it with several others. It is good for those who want to withdraw from the world or get married, and succeed in all things, because the Holy Spirit will lead them by the virtue of this Psalm. It is also useful for prisoners, by doing what is prescribed in Psalm 141.

Note that we must not persuade ourselves that the ungodly, the unbelieving, the scoffers, the proud, the greedy, the liars and other sinners, or people shrouded in the darkness of vice, of ignorance, and of all other human passions, can taste the fruits of a divine tree; because if some curious wanted to experience it to satisfy his curiosity, his pleasures, his revenge, his avarice, his vanity and other passions, and that he does not succeed according to his desires, he must not attribute the fault to this so holy work, but only to himself who made himself unworthy by his crimes, because this grace so admirable and so particular is reserved only for those who are truly people of good, and filled with charity, piety, humility, and all the other divine virtues. (Fig.7)

ENCHIRIDION

OF POPE LEO

Sent as a rare present to the Very Serene
Charles-the-Great, *Emperor.*

SAINT Leo, Pope, has collected and put in order the following Orison from the very words and precepts of our holy Mother Church, and sent it to Charlemagne, saying: If you firmly believe, without doubting, that each day you will recite the following Orison, with devotion, and carry it with you with respect, either in the home, whether in war, or at sea or wherever you may be, none of your enemies will have advantage over you; you will be invincible and delivered from the most wicked infirmities and adversities. In the name of Our Lord Jesus Christ, so be it.

And in favour and memory of the same King Charles, he had it written in letters of gold, which he always carried with great care and the utmost respect and devotion. Thus no mortal can express the virtues of this Orison. If men knew its excellence and virtue, they would recite it every day with great devotion, and would never remove it from them, especially as there is no one in the world who, having recited it, has been abandoned by God in all his needs and necessities, and has not come to his goal, ending his days happily; the incontestable experience has made it known to many, as well as to those who will recite it each day with devotion, and will carry it with honour and respect, without any alteration of body, to the glory and praise of God Almighty, of the glorious Virgin Mary his Mother, and of all the heavenly Court, will be preserved during this day for iron, water, fire and sudden death. Even the Devil will have no power over him nor will he die without confession. His enemy will have no advantage over him, either while sleeping, neither in nor out of the path, nor in any place whatsoever. He will never be defeated nor taken prisoner. It is also marvellous against storms, lightning and thunder; if recited over a vase of holy water, sprinkled on the air in the shape of a cross, at once the storm and thunder will cease. If one is at sea and recite it three times, no unfortunate accident or storm will occur on that day; being also said three times over a person possessed by a malignant spirit, either for himself or by someone else, by the light of a blessed candle, he will be instantly delivered. If a woman is in peril during the course of labour work, and the aforementioned Orison is recited three times by the light of a blessed candle, she will be delivered at once: and if someone wants to leave and go on a journey, let him say it also three times before setting out, or recite it before him and carry it with him on

his journey, he will be delivered from all accidents and sins; and if he dies of any illness,
he will be saved.

This trustworthy Orison has been tried
and tested by many people.

Here begins the mysterious Orisons of
Pope Leo.

*Orison against all kinds of charms, enchant-
ments, spells, characters, visions, illusions,
possessions, obsessions, impediments, bane
of marriage, and all that can come to us by
the curses of sorcerers, or by the incursions of
Devils, and also very profitable against all
kinds of misfortunes that can be given to
horses, mares, oxen, sheep, and such other
species of animals.*

WORD who was made flesh, tied to a cross, seated on the right side of God the Father, I beseech thee by thou holy Name, at the pronunciation of which every knee bend, hear the prayers of those who put their trust and belief in thou, deign to preserve this creature N., by thy Holy Name, by the merits of the holy Virgin thy Mother, by the prayers of all the saints, yes saints of God, from any attack of evil from demons

and malignant spirits, thou who live and reign
with God the Father and the Holy Spirit in
unity. For this is the Cross of Our Lord Jesus
Christ, on which depends our salvation, our
life, our spiritual resurrection, and the con-
fusion of all demons and evil spirits. Flee
therefore, vanish from here, demons, sworn
enemies of men; for I conjure thee infernal
demons, malignant spirits, whoever thou may
be, present or absent, under whatever pretext
thou may be called, invited, conjured or sent
of thy own free will, or forced by threats or
by the artifice of wicked men or women, to
dwell or inhabit here: I conjure thee therefore again, however obstinate thou may be,
to leave this creature by the great living God
† by the true God † by the Holy God † by
God the Father † by God the Son † and by
the Holy Spirit, who is also God † but main-
ly by him † who was immolated in Isaac †
sold in Joseph † who being man was crucified
† who was slain as a lamb, by whose blood

Saint Michael fighting with thee, defeated thee, made thou flee, when thou wanted to appear before him; I forbid thee on his part and by his authority, under any pretext whatsoever, to do any harm to this creature, either in its body or out of it, neither by vision, nor fright nor fear, both night and day, whether it sleeps, its awake, eats, prays, or acts naturally or spiritually: I mean by this, if thou are rebellious to my will, I throw upon thee all curses, excommunications, and condemn thee on behalf of the Most Holy Trinity to go into the lake of fire of brimstone where thou will be led and tormented, by the blessed Saint Michael; for if thou have been obliged to do so, either by some strong and express commandment, or by some cult of worship and perfume, or by some spell cast by word or magic, either on grass, on stones or in the air, whether that which was done naturally, simply, mixed, whether these things are temporal or spiritual, or whether sacred things have been used, whether the names of the great God or of the Angels have been used, whether one has made use of the Characters, has examined the hours, minutes, days, years, even months, or any tacit or manifest pact has been made with thee, even with a solemn oath. I break, destroy and cancel all these things by the power and virtue of God the Father † who created all things, by the wisdom of the Son † Redeemer of all men, by the goodness of the Holy Spirit †; in a word, by Him who fulfilled the Law in its entirety † who is †, was † and always will be *omnipotens Agios † Athanatos † Sother † Tetragrammaton † Jeova † Alpha & Omega † begining and end*; in a word, may all infernal power be destroyed and put to flight, by making on this creature N. the sign of the Cross on which Jesus Christ died, and by the incarnation of the Holy Angels, Archangels, patriarchs, prophets, apostles, martyrs, confessors, virgins, and of the blessed Virgin Mary, and generally of all the saints who have enjoyed the presence of God since the creation of the world, as well as of the holy souls who live saintly in the Church of God. Pay thy homage to the most high and mighty God, and that they reach to his throne, as the smoke from the heart of that fish which was burned by the order of the Archangel Raphael; disappear as the foul spirit disappeared from before the chaste Sara; may all these blessings drive thee away and not allow thee to approach in any way this creature who has the honour of bearing on his forehead the sign of the Holy Cross, because the command I give thee now is not mine, but the one sent from the bosom of the Eternal Father, in order to annihilate and destroy thy evil spells, which he did by suffering death on the tree of the Cross. He gave us this power to command thee, thus by his glory, for the good of the faithful; thus we forbid thee, according to the power we received from Our Lord Jesus Christ and in his name, to approach this creature: flee therefore, disappear at the sight of the Cross; the lion of the tribe of Judah conquered, as did the family of David: Alleluia. So be it, so be it. Let it be done, let it be done.

B Y whom, O Lord, you always produce
all these goods † you sanctify † vivify
and bless them † it is through himself † with
himself † and in himself, which to you God
Almighty Father belongs all honour, glory,
strength and power, for ever and ever. So be
it. Let us pray, being instructed by the command of the Saviour, and being led by divine
institution, we dare to say:

For Sunday.

O UR Father, who art in heaven, hallowed
be thy Name; thy kingdom come, etc.,
but deliver us from evil. So be it.

Please deliver me, Lord, who am your
creature N., from all evils, past, present and
to come, both of the soul and body, and by

your goodness give me peace and health, and be propitious to me, as I am your creature, through the intercession of the blessed Virgin Mary and your apostles, Saint Peter, Paul, Andrew, and all the saints. Grant peace and health to your creature during my life, so that being assisted by the help of your mercy, I may never be a slave to sin, nor in fear of any trouble, through the same Jesus Christ your Son, our Lord, who being God, lives and reigns in the unity of the Holy Spirit for ever and ever. So be it. May the peace of the Lord be with me always, so be it. May this heavenly peace, O Lord, which you left to your disciples, always remain firm in my heart, and always be between me and my enemies, both visible and invisible, so be it. May the peace of the Lord, his face, his body, his blood, help, comfort and protect me, your creature N., as well as my soul and my body, so be it. Lamb of God, who deigned to be born of the Virgin Mary, who on the Cross washed the world of its sins, have mercy on my soul and my body; Christ, Lamb of God, immolated for the salvation of the world, have mercy on my soul and my body. Lamb of God, through whom all the faithful ones are saved, give me your peace, which must last forever, both in this life and the next. So be it.

For Monday.

O GREAT God, through whom all things have been delivered, deliver me also from all evil! O great God, who granted your consolation to all beings, grant it to me too! O great God, who rescued and assisted all things, help me too and rescue me in all my necessities, my miseries, my undertakings, my dangers; deliver me from all the oppositions and snares of my enemies, both visible and invisible, in the name of the Father who created the whole world † in the name of the

Son who redeemed it † in the name of the Holy Spirit who fulfilled the law in all its perfection; I throw myself entirely into your arms, and place myself entirely under your holy perfection, so be it. May the blessing of God the Almighty Father, the Son and the Holy Spirit be with me always, so be it. † May the blessing of God the Father, who with his word alone made all things, be always with me. † May the blessing of Our Lord Jesus Christ, son of the great living God, be with me always, † so be it. May the blessing of the Holy Spirit with his seven gifts always be with me, † so be it. May the blessing of the Virgin Mary with her Son be always with me, so be it. May the blessing and consecration of the bread and wine that Our Lord Jesus Christ made when he gave them to his disciples, saying to them:

TAKE and eat of this, all of you: This is my body, which shall be given up for you in remembrance of me and for the remission of all sins, be with me always. † May the blessing of the Holy Angels, Archangels, Virtues, Powers, Thrones, Dominations, Cherubim, Seraphim be always with me, † so be it. May the blessing of the patriarchs and prophets, apostles, martyrs, confessors, virgins, and all the saints of God be always with me, † so be it. May the blessing of all God's heavens be always with me, † so be it. May the majesty of God Almighty sustain and protect me; may his eternal goodness lead me; may his boundless charity inflame me; may his supreme divinity lead me; may the power of the Father preserve me; may the wisdom of the Son vivify me; may the virtue of the Holy Spirit always be between me and my enemies both visible and invisible, so be it. Power of the Father, strengthen me; wisdom of the Son, enlighten me; consolation of the Holy Spirit, comfort me. The Father is peace, the Son is life, the Holy Spirit is the remedy of consolation and salvation, so be it. May the divinity of God bless me, so be it; may his piety warm me; may his love preserve me. O Jesus Christ, Son of the great living God, have mercy on me, a poor sinner.

For Wednesday.

O EMMANUEL! defend me against the evil enemy and against all my enemies visible and invisible, and deliver me from all evil. Jesus Christ the King came in peace: God made man, who suffered patiently for us. May Jesus Christ the good King always be in the midst of me and my enemies to defend me, so be it. Jesus Christ triumphs † Jesus Christ reigns † Jesus Christ commands

†. May Jesus Christ deliver me from all evils, continually, so be it. May Jesus Christ deign to give me the grace to triumph over all my adversaries, so be it. Behold the Cross of Our Lord Jesus Christ. Flee then, my enemies, at the sight of it, the lion of the tribe of Judah has triumphed; race of David, alleluia, alleluia, alleluia, Saviour of the world, save me, and help me, you who redeemed me by your Cross and your most precious Blood; come to my aid, I beseech you, my God, O Agios † Otheos † Agios Ischyros † Agios Athanos † Eleison Himas. Holy God, strong God, merciful and immortal God, have mercy on me who am your creature N.; be my support, Lord, do not abandon me; do not reject my prayers; God of my salvation, always be at my aid, God of my salvation.

ENLIGHTEN my eyes with a true light, so that they are not closed with an eternal sleep, lest my enemy have reason to say that I had the advantage over him. As long as the Lord is with me, I shall not fear the malignity of my enemies. O most gentle Jesus, preserve me, help me, save me; may every knee bow at the mere mention of the name of Jesus, whether heavenly, earthly or infernal, and may every tongue speak that Our Lord Jesus Christ enjoys the glory of His Father, so be it. I know, without a doubt, that as soon as I call upon the Lord on any day and at any hour, I shall be saved. Most gentle Lord Jesus Christ, Son of the great living God, who did such great miracles by the power of your most precious Name alone, and enriched the needy so abundantly, since by his power demons must flee, the blind see, the deaf hear, the lame walked upright, the dumb spoke,

lepers cleansed, the crippled healed, the dead
rose; for as soon as this most gentle name of
Jesus was pronounced, the ear was charmed
and delighted, and the mouth filled with the
most pleasing things: at this one pronunciation, I say, the demons fled, every knee bent,
even all temptations; the most evil were up-
rooted; all infirmities healed, all the disputes
and fights that are and were between the
world, the flesh and the devil were dissipated,
and one was filled with all heavenly goods;
because whoever invoked and will invoke this
Holy Name of God was and will be saved;
this Holy Name pronounced by the Angel
even before it was conceived in the womb of
the Blessed Virgin.

For Friday.

O GENTLE Name! Name that strengthens
the heart of man; Name of life, salva-

tion and joy; Name that is precious, rejoicing, glorious and pleasing; Name that strengthens the sinner; Name that saves, leads, governs and preserves all. May it please us then, most pious Jesus, by the power of this very most precious Name, remove the devil from me; enlighten me, Lord, for I am blind; dispel my deafness; straighten me for I am lame; give me back my speech, for I am mute; heal my leprosy; restore health to me, for I am sick; and resurrect me, for I am dead; give me back my life and surround me on all sides, both within and without, so that being equipped and strengthened with this Holy Name, I may live forever in you, praising and honouring you, because all is due to you, because you are the most worthy of glory: the Lord is the eternal Son of God, through whom all things rejoice and are governed. Praise, honour and glory be yours forever and ever, so be it. May Jesus always be in my heart, in my entrails, so be it. May Our Lord Jesus Christ always be within me, that he may restore me; may he be around me, that he may preserve me; may he be before me, that he may lead me; may he be behind me, that he may guard me; may he be above me, that he may bless me; may he be within me, that he may vivify me; may he be with me, that he may govern me; may he be above me, that he may strengthen me; may he be with me always, that he may deliver me from all the pains of eternal death, he who lives and reigns with the Father and the Holy Spirit for ever and ever. So be it.

For Saturday.

JESUS, Son of Mary, salvation of the world, may the Lord be favourable to me, gentle and propitious, may he grant me a holy and willing spirit to restore the honour and respect due to him, who is the liberator of the world. No one can lay a hand

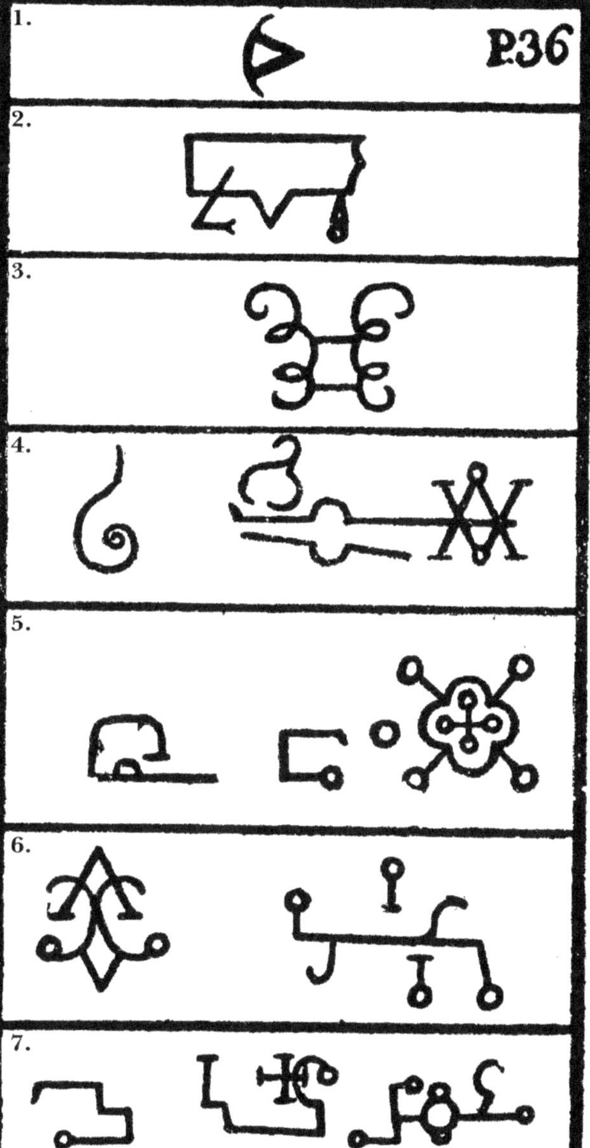

on him, because his hour had not yet come, he who is, who was and who always will be, was God and Man, beginning and end; may this prayer I make to him guarantee me eternally against my enemies. So be it. Jesus of Nazareth, King of the Jews, honourable title, Son of the Virgin Mary, have mercy on me, poor sinner, N., lead me according to your gentleness in the way of eternal salvation. So be it. Jesus, knowing the things that were to happen to him, came forward and said to them: Whom do you seek? They answered him: Jesus of Nazareth. Jesus said to them, I am he. Judas, who was to betray him, was with them, and as soon as he told them it was him, they fell back, dropping to the ground. Then Jesus asked once again: Whom do you seek? They said to him: Jesus of Nazareth. Jesus answered: I have already told you that I was he. If it is me that you seek, let these go (speaking of his disciples). The spear, the nails, the cross, the thorns, the death I suffered prove that I have erased and atoned the crimes of the miserables : preserve me, Lord Jesus Christ, from all wounds, poverty and the snares of my enemies, let the five wounds of Our Lord serve me continually as a remedy; Jesus is the way † Jesus is the life † Jesus is the truth † Jesus suffered † Jesus was crucified † Jesus, son of the living God, have mercy on me †. Now, Jesus passing by went among them, and no one laid his murderous hand on Jesus, because his hour had not come.

Mysterious Orison.

I CONJURE all of you, saints, martyrs, confessors and virgins of God, to intercede Our Lord Jesus Christ for me, a poor sinner, who lives and reigns eternally with the Holy Spirit, to make me enjoy his Holy Paradise, so be it. May the God of Abraham † God of Isaac † God of Jacob † of Aaron † of Elijah † God of Noah †; and finally, may this God, I say, always be with me, so be it. Blessed Angels Saint Michael, Saint Raphael, Gabriel, the Archangel, Cherubim and Seraphim, all the holy Angels and Archangels, and may all the saints come to my aid for all the days of my eternal life, so be it. Amedan † Austos † Taustazo † Barachedio † Memor † Gedita † Eleison † Maton † Igion † Frigam † Fides † Valey † Unis † Regnat † Sadau † Hagios † Otheos † Sanctus Deus † Hagios † Athanatos

† Eleïson † Himas † Saint Immortal, have mercy on me, a poor sinner, so be it. † Blessed Saint Michael Angel † Raphael † Uriel † Gabriel † Barachiel † Cherubim † and Seraphim † intercede for me with God; behold † the Cross of Our Lord Jesus Christ. Flee, then, my enemies; the lion of the tribe of Judah has conquered; race of David, alleluia. O God, deliver me from my enemies and from the hands of those who do evil, and from those who would soak their hands in my blood, so be it. O God, make the glory of your Name shine forth, and save me, and make your power appear, upholding the goodness of my cause. † You who save Kings, who redeemed David your servant, deliver me from the sword of my enemies who maliciously seek to do me harm. Jesus Christ conquers † Jesus reigns † Jesus Christ commands † may Jesus Christ preserve and defend me from all evil, so be it.

Orison against the adversities of the world.

HE will break the bow, shatter the weapons and throw the shields into the fire. Let them rest, he says, and acknowledge my power and divinity; my glory will shine among the nations and I will be glorified in all the earth, so be it.

To the Virgin.

MAKE us feel that you are the Mother, by granting our prayers, to the one who was willing to be your son to redeem us.

A very effective Orison.

THE right hand of the Lord has shown all his strength, the right hand of the Lord has shown his power by lifting me up, the right hand of the Lord has showed all his power; life will not be taken from me, but on the contrary, I will live and tell the wonders of the Lord. The Lord has punished me with his justice, he has chastised me because of my crime, but his goodness has delivered me from death. So be it.

When my enemies drew near to harm me and pounced on me like wild beasts on prey to devour it. At the same time as they made their persecution felt, God made them feel their weakness, and they fell into the traps they had set to harm me.

P.42
P.42

Orison of great virtue.

O THEOS, God, glorify your name and save me. Agios, as soon as I have confessed my crime to you and no longer keep my offences secret. Holy Holy Holy open my mind and teach me to adore, glorify and praise you. Otheos, Eleison: let those who outrage me feel the effect of your justice, Almighty Lord: annihilate, Lord, those who come forward to attack me: Messias, Soter, Emmanuel, which means God with us, ready your weapons, take up your shield and save me: Jesus, rise up to rescue me; bread, flower, light, praise, spear, spirit, door, stone, rock, Athanatos, draw the sword in my favour; Ischyros, decide the doom of those who persecute me; Jesus, my Saviour, make them unable to defend themselves, support my soul and assure me that you want to save it. True Panton, Pantastron,

Craton, Sabahot, do not abandon me to the fury of my enemies and save me from those who rise on all sides with the intention of harming me. My Lord, give in to my prayers, come and deliver me from those who afflict and slander me. Consider, my God, the evils I suffer justly for my sins; deign to cleanse me of my sins; hasten, and purify me so with your grace that it extinguishes in me the spirit of fornication, and that it inflames me continually to do good, which I beseech you to grant me by the strength and virtue of God the Father; of God the Son and of God the Holy Spirit, who are eternal and without end. Reign for ever and ever, so be it. *Pater* and *Ave* must be said entirely.

Orison.

THE Lord is merciful and forgiving, he waits a long time for sinners to do penance, and his bounties are infinite; he is great, as well as terrible: I make a sincere confession of my faults to you; I uncover my wounds to you; I beseech your ineffable goodness to kindly forget my sins and the miseries I have committed against you, since you were kind enough to say that you did not want the sinner to die, but rather to convert and live, so be it. I confess, I have sinned, I have even sinned in your presence; my life is but a tissue of sins and miseries; in a word, my soul is as if drowned and extinguished in the great number of iniquities; namely, pride, sloth, avarice, lust, anger, impatience, malice, envy, gluttony, drunkenness, evil de-sires, theft, perjury, loose talk, impertinences, ignorance, negligence and an infinite number of other sins that have given death to my soul; my heart is corrupted and infected, my lips, my sight, my hearing, my taste, my smell and my tact or touch in every way, by words, thoughts and actions; yet, I apprehend nothing when I have the happiness of being in your divine presence.

I beseech you most earnestly, O my God, whose compassion knows no bounds, deliver me from my miserable infirmities and forgive me in the same way you forgave the sinful woman: allow me, Lord, to give you the kiss of peace, as you allowed her to continually kiss your sacred feet, to water them with her tears, to wipe them with her hair. Grant me the grace to have a love for you as extensive as the number of my sins against your divine Majesty, so that in favour of your infinite mercy you may forgive me them all; deign also to grant me the forgiveness of my former faults and the grace not to commit any more in the future; also grant me the grace to obtain entirely your divine mercy before I die, and do not allow me to expire or end my days, that you have not granted me the complete forgiveness of my sins. But since I am a miserable sinner and you are so good as to forgive me, I give you infinite praise and thanks, O my God, who by your infinite mercy made me in your image and likeness and deigned (by regenerating me with the sacred waters of baptism) to adopt me and make me one of your dear children.

I give you infinite praise and thanks for having preserved my life from childhood to this moment; you are still so good as to wait for me, as a result of your infinite mercy, to come to terms with this infinite number of sins I have committed against your divine majesty: my expressions are too weak to return to you, O my God, the praise and glory you deserve for pointing such a benefit that, by your excessive goodness, have very often delivered me from my frequent tribulations, unfortunate situations, calamities and miseries in which I have found myself, who have until now preserved me from eternal torments, as well as from the tortures of the body.

I reiterate my most humble actions of praise and glory to you, who by your pure goodness have kindly granted me health of the body, tranquillity of life, good movements and finally charity; in a word, if I possess them, I am indebted to your infinite mercy: please grant me, my God, the priceless gift of your gentleness and increase in me the good you have been kind enough to grant me and banish from me all that displeases you therein; cleanse me and deliver me from my tribulations, and generally from all the various evils that surround me, and please regulate according to your holy will my thoughts, words and actions and make me always joyful and happy, even in the midst

of my adversities and that you conform my
desires at all times to your holy will, you who
live and reign eternally. So be it.

For human frailty.

H OLY God † strong † and immortal and
merciful † my Saviour, do not allow
us to be exposed to a death † untoward and
cruel; remember this society which belongs
to you, for all eternity.

Orison.

O God, who knows that we are exposed to so many perils and dangers, and that we cannot subsist because of our human frailty, please grant us salvation to the body and soul, deliver us by your help, we, whom you justly punish because of our sins; we beseech you through Our Lord Jesus Christ. So be it.

Orison against one's enemies.

Now, Jesus, passing through the midst of them, went his way: may the Lord be blessed from day to day, and as he is our Saviour, he will lead us happily in the way he has marked out for us †; now, Jesus, that darkness blind them, without their being able to have the use of their eyes, and may, as a mark of their unworthiness, always be bowed down to the Earth †; now, Jesus, pour upon them the effects of your indignation and may your righteous anger give them continual alarms †: may horror and dread strike down their courage in the mere idea of your strength. Do, Lord, let them become motionless as stones until I, N., who am your creature whom you redeemed with your precious blood, have passed †. Lord, the strength of your arm has marvellously signalled itself ; it will exterminate by its force a powerful enemy, lowering the pride of the impious who rise against me. † Deliver me, Jesus, and save me from those who rise on every side with the intention of harming me. † Lord Jesus, keep me from the hands of the wicked and take me away from those of unjust men, † Deliver me, Jesus, from the hands of those who commit evil; save me and defend me from those who seek to spill my blood. †

Glory be to the Father; to the Son, to the Holy Spirit, today and forever, in all ages of ages, as it was from the beginning and in all eternity. So be it.

Orison.

O Lord Jesus Christ, son of the great living God, who at the hour of your most Sacred Passion said to those who were looking for you: Whom are you looking for? At these words, they were overthrown and fell to the ground; deign, I beseech you, to deliver me, in the same way, from my enemies and their evil intentions, saying to them: Let N. go unharmed, this one who is my creature, and may they do me no harm at any time, either now or in the future: you who live and reign with God the Father in the unity of the Holy Spirit. So be it.

A very useful Orison for those who travel.

O GLA † Pentagrammaton † On † Athanatos † Anasareon † On † Pentareon † door † Croix † Agratam, † flock † light † Teta tustus † of man † Tomon † Tetragrammaton † Jesus † God † Lord of all things † Merciful † Most High † my Lord, deliver me N. who am your creature, deliver me, I say, by all these holy names, who have recourse to you, you my God who is everywhere, remember. Lord, from all your bounties, and deliver me from the snares of my enemies, both visible and invisible, I ask you, Lord, by the strength and virtue of this holy Cross, † and by the merits of all your saints. Now Jesus passing through the midst of them, went his way. † Jesus Christ, son of the great living God, † have mercy on me.

*Admirable Orison of the Cross
of the Saviour.*

† Cross of Jesus Christ, save me. † Cross of Jesus Christ, protect me. † Cross of Jesus Christ, preserve me from all evil, may those who offend me feel the effect of your justice. † Almighty God, annihilate those who come forward to attack me. † God Messiah, † God of hosts † Sother † Emmanuel, take your weapons and your shield. God of hosts, Our Lord Jesus Christ, pull me out of the mud, that I may not perish. † Holy God, deliver me from the hatred of my enemies. † Eli, deliver me from the depths of the waters that surround me. † O our salvation, make sure I do not descend into the abyss of the sea. † O Athanatos, let me not feel the violence of the fire. † O our resource, let not the taint of the in-

fernal well infect my mouth nor my sense of smell, † but you, my deliverer, open my mouth and exterminate my enemies. † O Athanatos, tell my soul that you want to save it. † Tetragrammaton, do not abandon me to the fury of my enemies. † Adonay, save me from those who rise on all sides to harm me. † Jesus, Saviour of the world, save me, † living bread, immutable flower, † strength and gateway to Paradise. † May the blessing of the Blessed Virgin Mary be upon me always with her Son, † may the blessing of Our Lord Jesus Christ and holy apostles be upon me, † and may the blessing of the Holy Spirit be upon me, † may the blessing of God the Almighty Father be upon me with his holy Angels and saints. † May the blessing of the Holy Trinity, the Father, the Son and the Holy Spirit, be upon me. † May the blessing of Saint Catherine of Mount Sinai be upon me, † May the blessing of all the holy Angels, Archangels, patriarchs, prophets, apostles,

evangelists, martyrs, all the virgins, monks
and pontiffs be upon me.

Orison to the Blessed Virgin.

HAIL, glorious Virgin, Star brighter than
the Sun, ruddier than the new Rose,
whiter than the Lily, higher in Heaven than
any saint, all the Earth reveres you. Accept
my homage and help me with your divine assistance. So be it. *Pater* and *Ave* in entirety.

Exhorting to Jesus Christ.

H AGIOS, invisible Lord, deliver me, I humbly beseech you, from death, I beseech you by thy Name; Oston, deign to help me, poor sinner who has recourse only to you, † Tetragrammaton, you are the King of kings, God the Father, Lord of lords, and it is in you alone that I place my assurance, you who govern and regulate the things of Heaven and Earth; I beseech you to have compassion and take pity on me, who am a sinner, I beseech you again, I, N., to deliver me from all my enemies, Lord, that Geban, Suth and Sutan also have mercy on them, in the name of the Father † and of the Son † and of the Holy Spirit. So be it. The first Name of God is Oston, the second Orthon. And when God said let there be light, it was done at once: the third is Lophias † in the name of the Lord, and of the indivisible Trinity †, Antaciton † Ituriensis grin Adonay, save me, Chedes and Ei, and Dotheos Adonay. So be it.

Deliver me, Lord, by the Tau sign, †

IN the name of the Father, and of the Son, and of the Holy Spirit. So be it. In the name of the holiest and most individual Trinity. So be it. † I conjure you, whatever weapons there may be, knives, swords, arrows, tools that cut at both ends, spears, nails, and all other weapons even of metal, by the Father, the Son, and the Holy Spirit, that you may in no way injure me, N., nor shed my blood, until I have expressly commanded you three times to use those things which cut, saw and shed blood, while I hold them in my hand. Now, if all the weapons of my adversaries could serve them to wound me, I beg you earnestly to melt them by your virtue like wax, † I conjure you again, whatever kind of weapons you may be, by the iron spear which the soldier Longinus used to open the side of Our Lord Jesus Christ, from which came out blood and water, not to be able to wound or harm me, nor to spill my blood. N. † I conjure you again by the column where Our Lord Jesus Christ was bound and led before the Judge, not to wound me, nor to shed my blood. † I conjure you again, by the three nails that pierced the feet and hands of Our Lord Jesus Christ, not to wound me, nor mark me in any way with blood. †

I conjure you again, whatever weapons you may be, by the iron grill on which Saint Lawrence, martyr, was roasted, not to harm me, wound me, nor spill my blood. † I conjure you again, whatever type of weapons you may be, by the sword with which Saint Paul was beheaded, not to harm me, nor shed my blood. † I conjure you also, by the iron

bond with which Saint Agnes was held for two years and tormented, that you may not wound me nor spill my blood. †

I conjure you again with all kinds of weapons by the iron instrument with which blessed Agatha was suspended, that you may not wound me or spill my blood. I conjure you again all weapons, swords, knives, tools that cut by two ends, and generally all kinds of weapons, by the seventy-two names of God known to us, and by this immutable God who governs Heaven and Earth, and generally all things contained therein, give him eternal glory. † I conjure you also by the Holy Name of God Fimandolum, by whose strength Joshua defeated twelve kings. † I conjure you also by the Holy Name of God Tetragrammaton. † Jot † Set † Neor † Nain † He, † I conjure you by all the joys and sorrows of the Blessed Mary ever Virgin. † I conjure you also by all the apostles, evangelists, martyrs, and by the twenty-four elders, by all the doctors, confessors, monks and hermits, by all the virgins and widows, by all the holy men and women of God, by the most holy oath of Our Lord Jesus Christ, by his true and sacred words by which no one even has the power or authority to offend, hurt, or even shed blood, † for I myself passing in the midst of them, will say: behold † the Cross of the Lord; vanish then, my enemies, and flee, the lion of the tribe of Judah has vanquished the race of David, † deliver us, Lord, from your enemies, by virtue of the sign of the Cross, † Precious Cross, I conjure you to receive me, and preserve from my enemies by him who has been set upon you, spirit of wisdom and understanding, † spirit of counsel and strength, † spirit of science † and piety, † spirit of fear of Our Lord, defend me and protect me from all weapons, and even from their wounds, from the wound of all swords, spears, bolts, arrows, and generally from the wound of all weapons, whatever they may be.

I conjure you to preserve me from them, I who am your creature N. † save me, † bless me, † sanctify me, † and guarantee me from all wounds by the sign † of your Holy Cross, † I conjure you by your five wounds, † Hely, † Eloy, † Het, † Clavis, † Egon, † Eth, † Huc, † Proth, ℞ † Ceretas, † A † Feros, † Homo, † the King of glory comes in peace, † the Word was made flesh (and dwelt among us : and we have seen the glory of God, as the only Son of the Father), it was full of grace and truth.

===================================

Orison to make a woman faithful
Adonay, Jod. Magister dicit Jo.

O GOOD Jesus! hear me, Emmanuel, Emmanuel, Sathor, Jessé adorable Tetragrammaton, Héli, Héli, Héli, Læbe Hey Hamy, this is my body, Tetragrammaton, come to my assistance now and at all times, † Jesus is victorious, † Jesus reigns, † Jesus commands, ℟ may Jesus Christ preserve me from all misfortune and lead me eternally to good fortune. So be it. You shall not fracture him, nor the arrows that are shot during the day; nor the pitfalls that are erected during the darkness, nor the attacks of the Demon who fights at high noon, a thousand fight- ers shall fall at your side, and ten thousand at your right hand, but none shall come near you, and let my enemies be confounded, but do not allow me, Lord, to be so: let them dry

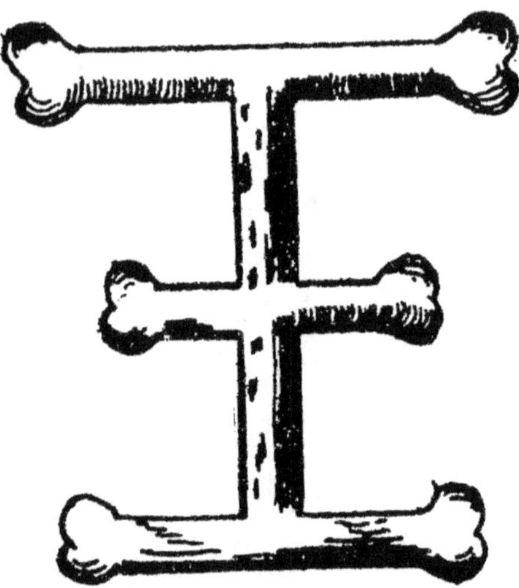
P.65
ADONAYJOB
MAGISTER
DICIT XCI

up with fear, but not me. O my God, make them feel your vengeance, and make them repent doubly. † Now, Jesus passing through the midst of them, went his way: and I will pass through the midst of them upheld by the great name Adonay †, now, Jesus passing through the midst of them, went without being seen; my God, I beseech you to make me this day and even while I live, to pass through the midst of my enemies without any danger, both to my soul and to my body. † If then it is I you seek, let these go † as Our Lord Jesus Christ himself said these words from his own mouth, may he also deign to deliver and defend me from my enemies. † Forbid them, O Lord, to do me any fracture, nor any harm; flee then, my enemies and disappear † in the name of the Father, in the name of the Son † and of the Holy Spirit, † Alpha & Omega, have mercy on me, shut the mouth and heart of my enemies, let no man or woman or deceitful or envenomed tongue have the upper hand over me, nor let me feel any harm. O God, save me, N., for I am your servant hoping in you, and this in honour of your name, and deliver me from all peril and danger. So be it. ††† ††. Let horror and dread strike down their courage in the mere thought of your strength; do, Lord, let them become motionless as stones until your creature, whose master and protector you are, Lord, has passed; Lord, I commend my spirit into your hands, † if you seek me so let these go. †††. But you will make use, Lord, of sorrows and afflictions, as of a bit and bridle, to bring back to you those who behave like beasts, and stray from you. Saint Michael, Saint Gabriel, Saint Raphael, defend me and support me in the fight I have to sustain against my enemies, and deliver me from all peril. So be it. Deliver me, my God, from all my enemies, visible and invisible; do not abandon me, Lord, for I am your creature. Blessed Virgin Mary, deliver me from the snares of my enemies. Hail Mary, full of grace, † my Lord Jesus Christ, who delivered your apostle Saint Peter from prison, Saint Paul from Damascus, Saint John the Evangelist from boiling oil, also deign, Lord, to deliver and preserve me from all captivity. Most Holy Virgin Mary, deliver me from torment and prison by your virginal womb, pure and immaculate, and by your holy salutation, may your creature N. be blessed and delivered from all peril and captivity. † Agla, † Lacta, † Sancta and El, † Ischyros, † Heloy, † Ceophobus, † Sabaoth, † Heleyon, † Ja, † Tetragrammaton, † Ely, † Adonay, † Sadai, † Fiat, † Fiat, † Fiat, may darkness blind them without the use of their eyes, and may, as a mark of their unworthiness, always be bowed down to the Earth. When you see me overwhelmed by the excess of affliction and in danger of losing my life, I will not even fear all these dangers, because you are there, Lord, to deliver me from them, and you will be at my side. If it is I you seek, then let these go. Please receive me favourably, Lord, and leave my enemies confused, because you are my protector and my consolation. Honour to God the Father who from his goodness is willing to deliver me from them: † and that I have put all my consolation in the hope of your help and protection: † in Jesus Christ by his divine mercy, † may the peace of Our Lord Jesus Christ be always with me, with the veneration he has for his father. So be it. † For this is my body †† may they love it. So be it. † Behold the Cross of the Lord, vanish and flee, demons and evil spirits, my enemies; the lion of the tribe of Judah has won the victory, race of David. Alleluia, Alleluia, Alleluia. Deliver me, my God, by this sign of † my enemies and all evil. † Cross of Jesus Christ, help me, Cross of Jesus Christ, rescue me, † Cross of Jesus Christ, save me † Cross of Jesus Christ, defend me against all my enemies and from all peril and danger. Hagios,

† O Theos, † Hagios, † Ischyros, † Ragios, † Athanatos † Eleïson † Himas †† Jesus of Nazareth, King of the Jews, make the glory of your Name shine forth. So be it.

Eternal praise to God.

I PRESENT myself to you, my enemies, provided with the grace of God, his love, with
the humility of Jesus Christ who is God, with
the strength and the word of the Holy Spirit
who is also God, with the glorious banner
of the Cross, accompanied by the glorious
Virgin Mary, the purity of Abel, the help of
Noah, the faith of Abraham, the obedience
of Isaac, the innocence of Jacob, the patience
of Job, the gentleness of Moses, the holi-
ness of Aaron, the wisdom of Solomon, the
victory of Joshua, the justice of David, the
strength of Samson, the power of Peter, the
assurance of Paul, the chastity of John, the
word of Matthew, the contrition of Gregory,
the prayer of Clement, the splendour of the
Moon, the brightness of the Sun, and the
latitude of the Heavens, the longitude of the

Earth, the depth of the Sea, the course of the river Jordan, the glory of Holy Jerusalem, the help of all the saints and that of Our Lord Jesus Christ, through whom all things were made. May this same Son of God, who came from the Blessed Virgin Mary, enlighten my spirit with the light of glory, may he change the enmity of my enemies into love; may their evil will, their perverse intentions and their pernicious projects be annihilated by his gentleness, and may in virtue of all the holy names we have spoken of above, and that of the great Almighty God, all their efforts be useless and without effect; may this same God who was born of the blessed Virgin Mary change all your evil and diabolical thoughts into good and for my advantage. So be it. So be it. So be it. May Jesus Christ true God, full of tenderness and compassion for men, for whom he is the judge of the living and the dead; may the Holy Names of the Almighty God serve me as a most powerful shield and helmet against the envenomed darts of my enemies, so that they can do no harm to me N., for I am the creature of God; may they be rendered fusible at my approach like wax in the heat of fire. So be it. † Jesus Christ is victorious, † Jesus Christ reigns, † Jesus Christ commands, † may Jesus Christ deliver and preserve me from all adversities, and even from death, for I am his creature. So be it. †

Jesus Christ the King comes in peace, and God made man; now, Jesus, passing through the midst of them, went his way † everything is consumed, † whom do you seek † it is I; † if it is I that you seek, then let these go; † now, Jesus, passing through the midst of them, went his way † everything is consumed, † and bowing his head, the spirit is returned. Praise to God and to the Blessed Virgin Mary, God will destroy you, † he will take you away, † he will cast you out from your dwelling, he will uproot you from the land of the living to punish your malignity. In the name of the Father, † and of the Son, † and of the Holy Spirit, † So be it.

At the sole name of Jesus, may every knee bow, whether celestial, terrestrial, and even infernal, and may every tongue proclaim loudly that Our Lord Jesus Christ is at the right hand of God, the Father enjoying his glory: now, we must therefore glorify in the Cross of Our Lord Jesus Christ in which our salvation is found, our life, our spiritual resurrection, by which Jesus Christ has saved us all; may God pour upon us the almighty effects of his goodness, and may he fill us with his blessings; may he make the light of his countenance shine upon us, and may he help us with his mercy.

I T was found in Constantinople in a golden cross. Whoever wears it cannot have better protection than this. He cannot die from sudden death, neither by fire, nor by water, nor by arrows, nor by storms, nor by thunder, nor by venom; neither by evil spirits, nor by false judgments, nor false witnesses. Moreover, if a pregnant woman carries it on her person, invoking the grace of Our Lord Jesus Christ, she will have no peril or danger during childbirth.

P.74

*Copy of the letter from Abagare, King of
Edessa, written and sent to Jesus Christ
in Jerusalem by the courier Ananas.*

ABAGARE, Son of Thopathaeus, King of
Edessa, to Jesus our Saviour, who was
seen in Jerusalem: greetings.

I have heard here of your fame, and of
the great wonders you work, and cures you
perform, without the aid of remedies and
salutary herbs, that your word alone is suf-
ficient to restore sight to the blind, to make
the lame walk, to cleanse the lepers and drive
away unclean spirits, that you restore health
to those who are far from you, that you even
raise the dead; the word of such deeds has
persuaded me, either that you are a God
come down from Heaven, or that you are the
Son of God, to do such great things, which
has prompted me to write to you to beg you

to kindly transport yourself to my country, and restore my health which a long illness has taken away from me; I have heard that the Jews are irritated with you and are setting up ambushes; come to me, my town is not very large, but it is well equipped and strong enough to preserve you, and I salute you and recommend myself to you.

L ord, give me strength against my ene-
mies, answer my prayer, and let my cries reach up to you.

IN HOC SIGNO VINCES

*The words that are in the circle of the Pentacle
mean in English: In this sign, you will con-
vince. It is now necessary to exorcise and perfume the said Pentacle, then write the Orison which follows:*

*Response from Jesus Christ with an Orison of ad-
mirable virtues.*

BLESSED are you, King Abagare, for having believed in me, though you have not
seen me, for many have seen me, and yet did
not believed in me: as for what you write
me to go to you, I must accomplish here all
the things for which I was sent; after I have
completed them, I will send you one of my
disciples named Thaddaeus, that he may heal
your disease, and give life to you, and to all
who are with you; that is why I am sending
you this letter written by my hand, so that

wherever you find yourself, whether at home, on the sea, on the river or in battle against pagans or Christians, or in any other place, your enemies or adversaries will have no dominion over you, and you will have nothing to fear from the ambushes of the devil; foul spirits, lightning and thunder will not be able to harm you if you devoutly carry this prayer: I love you, O Abagare, and I promise you my salvation: may my peace be with you always.

Abagare having received this letter, read it and, with tears in his eyes, exclaimed: O Jesus Christ, Son of the living God! Almighty God, full of mercy, be propitious to me in all things, in the name of the holiest and most individual Trinity, the Father, the Son and the Holy Spirit; I conjure you (whatever weapons you may be) by the Father, the Son and the Holy Spirit; I conjure you, sticks, knives, spears, swords, daggers, arrows, clubs, ropes and all other kinds of weapons, by the seventy-two names of God, by his infinite virtue and supreme power; I conjure you by the spear with which the soldier Longin pierced the side of Jesus and it leaked blood and water, by the other Sacred Names of God, † Joth, † Hoet, † Vari, † Hei, † that you do not injure me N., who am the servant of God, and shed not my blood: I conjure you, all manner of weapons, by virtue of the Holy Names of God, † Hel, † Ya, † Hye, † Yae, Va, † Adonay, † Cados, † Oborel, † Eloym, † Agla, † Agiel, † Azel, † Sadon, † Esul, † Heloy, † Heloyn, † Delis, † Yeui, † Yacer, † Del, † Yosi, † Helim, † Rasaël, † Rasaël † Paliel, † Mamiel, Oncha, † Dilaton, † Xaday, † Alma, † Pavix, † Alim, † Catival, † Utauzaraf, † Zalfi, † Eala, † Carsaly, † Faffua, † Hictimi, † Sed, † Der, † Agla, † Aglaia, † Pamiel et Pannion, † Oniel, † On, † Homon, † Oreon, † Lestram, † Panteon, † Bamboy, † Ya, † Emmanuel, † Yoth, † Lucaf, † On, † Via, † Calip, † Lon, † Israël, † Miel, † Cyel, † Pyeel, † Patriteron, † Fafaron, †

Leuyon, Yael, † that you may not injure me
N., for I am the servant of God, nor shed
my blood. It is said, you shall not break his
bones, the right hand of the Lord has made
virtue, the right hand has exalted me; I shall
not die, but live and tell the wonders of the
Lord: the Lord has chastened me, but he has
not sent me to my death; praise and thanks
be to him. So be it.

The great Saint Leo, Pope, wrote to Charles, King of France, saying: Whosoever shall wear these holy names upon his person, he shall not be damaged by his mortal enemy, and it must be noted that in this is contained the name of Christ, which is Agla, which serves to be ice-shod against adversities, which being seen, it is said, worn daily, he shall not die of evil death.

IN the name of the Father, † and of the Son † and of the Holy Spirit. So be it. Rise, indivisible Trinity and unity, † one Messiah God † Sother † Emmanuel † Sabaoth † Adonay, † Coteraton † Ysion † Son † Lon † Con † Son † Osiam † Salvation † Life † Truth † Ve † Wisdom † I am † what I am † it is I who am the Lamb † the Sheep † the Calf † the Serpent † the Ram † the Lion † the Green † the Sun Agla † the Image † the Bread

† the Life † the Flower † the Mountain † the
Gate † the Fountain † the Pebble † the Stone
† the Angle † the Shepherd † the Prophet †
the Priest † the Saint † the Immortal † the
great King † I am the first † and the second
Lion † the third Flower † fourth Obise †
fifth Earth † sixth Premax † seventh Sagai †
eighth Bethlehem † ninth Tetragrammaton †
tenth Seloy † eleventh Eloy † Satos † Ecaton
† Himas — Eleïson † Saviour † Alpha † or
First † and Omega Last † the First Born † the
Beginning † the Comforter † the Mediator
† Word † Yschyros † the Glory † the Light
† the World † the Angular † the Holy † the
Immortal † Jesus the Father † Almighty Son
† Holy Spirit Mighty † Holy Merciful Spirit
† Eternal Whiteness or Purity † the Creator
† the Redeemer † the Angle of the Great
Council † Trin † a God † Holy, Holy, Holy,
the Lord of Lords, † the God of Gods † in-
effable God † incomprehensible † just Judge
† and always in battle, in the Sea, or in the

water, Gedebelone, S. E. Q. P. and always in the path in war: King of the Jews, have mercy on us: Alleluia. I beseech you, O my Lord God, Most Holy by all your Holy Names, and even entreat you to kindly answer my prayer, weak as it is, to kindly preserve me from all perils, vexations and the snares of the Devil, so as to deliver me from them, not only now, but even forever. God of Abraham, God of Isaac, God of Jacob, God of the Angels, God of the Apostles, God of the Martyrs, God of all the saints and chosen of God, please intercede God for me N., God, I say, so good, so gentle, so kind, so humble of heart, who does not wish the death of the sinner nor the loss of his soul.

Orison.

O God, whose mercy is infinite, I beseech you most earnestly by the power and virtue of all the holy names which are inserted or written in this book, and even in the name of all your holy saints, to please not only preserve me this day N., for I am your creature, but also at all times, as well as all your creatures, from all evil and iniquity, my friends and my enemies, and generally all the faithful ones who are on Earth. I beseech you with all the humility of which the human creature is capable, by the strength, virtue and merit of the death and passion of Our Lord Jesus Christ, by that of all your Holy Names; also by those of the Blessed Virgin Mary, and generally of all your holy saints, please preserve me today and always, wherever I may be, from the malignity of my enemies who only seek to do me wrong: preserve me, I say, generally from all perils, losses, thunders, storms, lightnings, pestilence, hunger, snakes, as well as from all evil and dangerous beasts, from peril of fire and water, of sudden and eternal death, so that we may all quietly and safely praise, bless and glorify you eternally unto the ages of ages. So be it. *Pater* and *Ave* entirely.

Save us from the hands of our enemies, so that having been delivered from their hands, we may serve you without fear. Lord, the strength of your arm has been marvellously demonstrated, you have exterminated a superb enemy, you have manifested the greatness of your glory, by lowering the pride of the impious who rose against you: the fire of your wrath that you sent down on their heads devoured them in an instant; the waters piled up one on top of the other, because they were aroused by the spirit of your fury; let horror and dread strike down their

courage, in the sole idea of your strength.
Do so, Lord, that they become motionless
as stones until your people have passed and
the people you have chosen are out of peril.
Jesus Christ, King of glory, has come; this
God made himself man, he withdrew with
an armed hand, and by the strength of his
almighty arm: now, Jesus passing through the
midst of them, went his way. Let horror and
dread strike down their courage in the sole
idea of your strength; do, Lord, that they become motionless as stones, until your people
have passed, and the people you have chosen
have passed.

*One must say this three times, when ready to pass
where lies the enemies; it is even said that
Charlemagne used it in war and thereby re-
mained invincible; from that time, people
had so much faith in the Orisons of the holy
Church that they avoided cannon fire by saying the following Orison:*

I ENTREAT you, Peter, through the blessed Saint Etienne, first martyr, whom the
accursed Jews stoned to death, who even
prayed for his persecutors and executioners,
saying Saint Jesus Christ, do not impute this
fault to them, rather deign to forgive them
(because they do not know what they are doing) so that you may not injure me N., for I
am the servant of God.

I CONJURE you, arrows, by the charity, scourging and freezing of Our Lord Jesus Christ, O arrow, remain without effect, I conjure you, by Heaven and Earth, the stars and the planets: be without effect, I conjure you, by the sepulchre of Our Lord Jesus Christ. O arrow, I command you by the resurrection of Our Lord Jesus Christ, not to harm anyone; O arrow, I conjure you once again, by Heaven, the Earth, the stars in the sky, and generally by all things that are in Heaven and on Earth, by the terrible and frightening day of universal judgment, by the virginity of the adorable body of Our Lord Jesus Christ, and by that of the glorious Virgin Mary, his Mother; not to harm anyone: O Arrow, I finally command and

order you by the Most Holy Trinity to remain without any effect.

May the peace of Our Lord Jesus Christ
be with me always, with the power of the
prophet Elijah: O arrow, do not kill, remain
without effect, I conjure you by the virtue of
the Blessed Virgin Mary, by the head of Saint
John the Baptist, by the twelve apostles, by the
four evangelists, by the martyrs, confessors,
virgins and widows of God, by the Angels
and Archangels: O arrow, I again make the
same defence to you by the great living God,
by the true God and by the holy God, by the
same God who made all things from nothing.
O arrow, I repeat the same defence to you by
the Annunciation of Our Lord Jesus Christ:
O arrow, once again, I forbid you to hurt or
harm me N., for I am the servant of God,
and by the ineffable memory of N. † 2 † I. †
q.g. 222. L. M. † I † Holy Jesus Christ, Alpha
† & Omega † Emmanuel, that no sword may
pierce me, that I may I be born by Our Lord

Jesus Christ my protector, my liberator and my saviour, may no iron have any effect on me, N., who am the servant of God.

Let those who revile me feel the effect of your justice. Annihilate, Lord, those who come forward to attack me; put on your weapons, take up your shield, arise to come to my aid and rescue, I, N., who am your servant, † so be it. † Tate Aiti † Ait Ain † may God preserve me from all evil and danger, from death, I, N., for I am the servant of God, so be it. J.C. conquers † J.C. commands † J.C. reigns † J.C. rules † J.C. leads † J.C. be in me; may he break and tear to pieces the iron that fights against me: O arrow, I command you by this spear of which I have made mention, I say, to remain without any effect that could be harmful to me, and that generally all the weapons of my enemies, both visible and invisible, have no effect on me, N., for I am the servant of God.

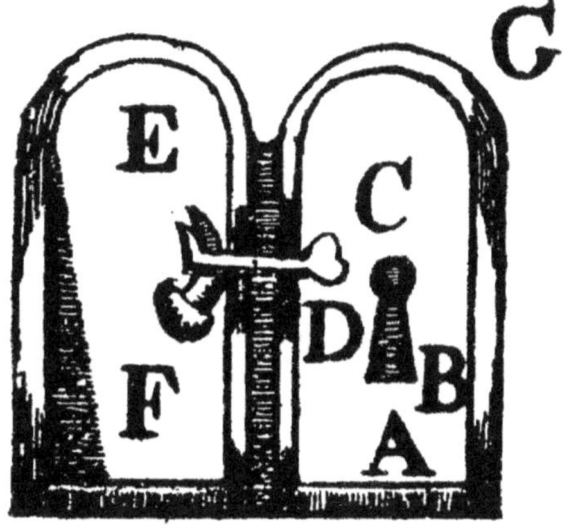
E
C
G
D
F
B
A

Whoever carries the aforementioned Orison on his person must fear nothing, either arrows, swords, or other weapons will not be able to harm him; neither the Devil, if he has not made a pact with him, nor magicians, nor any persons will be able to harm him; he will be safe in all places and always † † † . If one does not believe in this, let him venture, and he will see wonders: if he puts this Orison around his neck, nothing will harm him.

BARNASA † Leutias † Bucella † Agla † Agla † Tetragrammaton † Adonay † Lord God, great and admirable, help N. your servant, unworthy as I am † deliver me from all danger, from the death of the soul and of the body and from the snares of my enemies, both visible and invisible † God † Ely † Eloy † Ela † Adonay † Sabaoth † may these Holy Names † be profitable and salutary to me, N., for I am a servant of God † for this is my body, † may he love me. So be it.

There are ten names by which God is called in any place, and by which the body of Jesus Christ is said to be in some way forced and constrained. They are named in the Orison above.

Orison to conjure all kinds of weapons.

I CONJURE you, all kinds of weapons, which have contributed and served to kill all the holy martyrs, I command you to become without any effect, or rather forbid you by all their merits to have any nor power over me, to cut me in any part of my body whatsoever, nor even to spill any drop of my blood, nor to offend or wound me in any place what-soever, I, N., who am the servant of God; † Cross and Passion of Our Lord Jesus Christ, be in my memory, and give me against my enemies †, peace and blessing of Our Lord be always with me; O arrow, become useless to my enemies and without effect. I conjure you, by the virtue of the Blessed Virgin Mary, by the head of Saint John the Baptist, by the apostles, martyrs, confessors, virgins and widows, by the Angels and Archangels: † O arrow, I conjure you, by the crown of thorns which has been placed on the sacred head of Our Lord Jesus Christ † O arrow, I reiterate to you by the taking and scourging of Our Lord Jesus Christ † O arrow, from the nails which pierced the feet and hands of Our Lord Jesus Christ. O arrow, by the wounds of Our Lord Jesus Christ, by his resurrection, I forbid you from wounding me, N., who am the servant of God † in the name of the Father † and of the Son † and of the Holy Spirit. † So be it.

Orison.

PRIMA
SECŪDA
TERTIA
QUARTA
SERPENS

Orison to our Saviour, Jesus Christ.

I BESEECH you, Lord, Son of the great living God, by your Holy Cross, forgive my sins, keep my head safe by your Holy Cross, preserve my feet from all accidents by your invaluable Cross, and generally all my members; grant me, please, the forgiveness of my sins and eternal life. † Holy God, sanctify me † Almighty God, strengthen me † Eternal God, sustain me † Immortal God, have mercy on me, N., for I am your servant, because my sins are without number. I am not even worthy to be called your servant because of the offences I have committed against your divine Majesty; therefore I beseech you, O my God, to pour into my soul and heart your heavenly and divine love; you who live and reign eternally in Heaven and on Earth. So be it.

Another Orison.

MY God, my Father, have mercy on me † O Son, O Holy Spirit, be with me: deliver me from my enemies † sword, I conjure you, by the holy Priest of the Old Testament, who gave Mary entrance to the Temple and to Our Saviour Jesus Christ, saying: the sword of sorrow has penetrated to his soul, so that you may not wound me N., who am the servant of God: † I conjure you, you stones, by the blessed Saint Etienne, first martyr, whom the Jews stoned, not to wound me in any way whatsoever I, N., who am the servant of God. † In the name of the Father and of the Son, and of the Holy Spirit. So be it.

*Here are the words that Saint Leo, Pope, sent to
Charles, King of France and Emperor of the
West: Whoever carries them, reads them or
has them read to him, will have no misfortune on that day and will be preserved from
fire and water, will die in honour of old age
and will be provided for great offices; it will
be the same for a pregnant woman, who will
be relieved of them if she carries it on her.*

C ROSS of Jesus Christ which I always
adore † may the Cross of Jesus Christ
be my true salvation during my life and after
my death: † that the Cross of Jesus Christ
renders inoperative, against me, the sword
of my adversaries; † that the Cross of
Jesus Christ delivers me from the bonds of
Death; † that the Cross of Jesus Christ be
for me † a wonderful sign; † that the Cross
of Jesus Christ be my power, my might

and my strength; † that the Cross of Jesus
Christ be my safety, my safeguard, and assure me of favourable success against my
enemies; † may the Cross of Jesus Christ
deliver me from every peril, both present
and to come; † may I obtain the help of the
divine grace through this sign of the Cross,
and may its authority and power serve as my
barrier and defence against my enemies; †
may the Cross of Jesus Christ deliver me
from all the adversities and misfortunes of
this life; † may the Cross of Jesus Christ
always be with me and save me: may it be
before me, and behind me, because as soon
as the Devil, my ancient enemy, sees you before me and with me, he withdraws far away
and flees from me; † let all malignant and
evil spirits flee and avoid me by this sign of
the Cross † peace Heloy † Tetragrammaton
† Diday † Pontayeto Esbri † now, Jesus passing in the midst of them, went his way †
Jesus † Source † Principle † End † Truth †

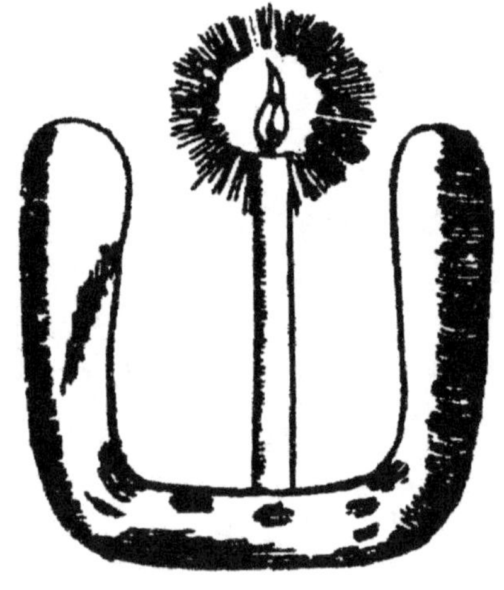

Almighty. † In the name of the Father † and
of the Son † and of the Holy Spirit. † So
be it.

*These are the names of Jesus Christ which are
chosen and taken from Holy Scripture, and
if anyone carries them, he will have all good
success and will lose nothing; also wearing
them hanging around the neck, they make
one loved by everyone.*

† A UTHOS, † a Nostro † Noxio, † Bay,
† Gloy, † Apen, † Agia, † Agios, †
Hischiros.

These are the words that Adam said, when he was in Hell or limbo, on the banks of the Acheron; if anyone in war carries them, he will not be killed there by any; same for the traveller who carries them the space of 70 days, he will not be caught on the way, nor attacked by thieves, and will have time to have a priest to hear his confession, and have remission of his sins: it is also of great virtue for those who travel by Sea. It wards off danger to those who wear it with great devotion.

† VALEAM da Zazac † Adonay N. † † † † † †. Beginning † and End † Unction † Wisdom † Truth † Hope † Comforter † it is I who am the Fountain † the Mediator † Agios † the Sheep † the Link † the Foot † the Lion † the Bread † Telos † the Hand † the Pebble † the Cornerstone † the Benefactor † the Husband † the Little one † the Divinity † the Veredic † the Darkness † the Grace † the Truth † the Peace † the Source † Atitay

† the Love † Alleluia † Alleluia † Alleluia. † So be it. † The Unity, the Strength † the Last † the Almighty † Matthew † John † Mark † Luke † † †.

Let these holy names be for the salvation of my soul in the name of Jesus, Mary, and in the name of Saint Eloy, as King Fabricius bore them, and left them to the King who was named Eloy, and so one cannot be taken or killed; if one does not wish to experience it on oneself, put them on an ox that the butcher wants to kill, never will he succeed.

PATHAY † Vey † Adonay † in the name of the Father † and of the Son † and of the Holy Spirit; † now, Jesus passing through the midst of them, went his way, † O † Var † Adar † Malarum terrarum negat † the Word was made flesh, and lived among us † Christus † Tetragrammaton † who said to him may it prosper thee. † So be it. Six † So be it. It is I who am this Jesus you seek. If you saw these people robbing my people, you would immediately run to be their friends, and you would make yourself the accomplice of adulterers: and nothing came out of your mouth but filth and malignity, and your tongue occupied itself only with skillfully deceiving those who trusted in you. † And pour out your blessings upon your inheritance. Praise God †.†.†.

CO MITY
DUCE FERIAE
DEO

*Orison of Saint Augustine addressed to the Holy
Spirit, that one will say to have revelation.*

O MY God, be propitious to me, I say,
who am but an unworthy and miserable sinner, deign to preserve me and be
with me continually throughout my life, both
night and day. God of Abraham. God of
Isaac, God of Jacob, have mercy on me, and
send me your holy Archangel Michael, to defend and protect me in all my troubles and
perils. Blessed Saint Michael, deliver me from
all perils, even from the terrible judgment of
God.

O blessed Saint Michael Archangel, I
beseech you by the grace you have merited,
through Our Lord Jesus Christ, only Son of
God, to deliver me today from the danger of
death. Saint Gabriel, Saint Raphael and all
the holy Angels of God, help me, I beseech

you all, as long as you are of heavenly virtue, to grant me your help and your power, so that none of my enemies, small or great, in a word, such as he may be, may not make me feel the effects of his malignity, nor of his vengeance, neither on the road, nor on the water, nor by fire, nor that he may procure me any sudden death, nor that he may, in a word, be contrary to me, whether I sleep, or remain awake.

Behold † the Cross of the Lord, flee then and vanish, you all my enemies, who seek to harm me, the lion of the tribe of Judah is victorious, race of David; Alleluia. Saviour of the world, save us, you who redeemed us by the shedding of your own blood on the tree of the Cross. We humbly beseech you, O God, to help us. Agios, Otheios, Agios, Ischyros, Agios, Athanatos, Eleïson Himas, holy God, strong God, immortal God, have mercy on us. Adorable Cross of Jesus Christ, save us; Cross of Jesus Christ, protect us;

Cross of Jesus Christ, defend us. In the name of the Father and of the Son and of the Holy Spirit. So be it.

P. 105

Orison of Saint Cyprian.

I, Cyprian, servant of Our Lord Jesus Christ, prayed to God the Almighty Father, and said to him: You alone are the strong God, my Almighty God who dwells in the heavens, a dwelling full of light, you are holy and praiseworthy, you foresaw from all eternity the wickedness of your servant, and the iniquities into which I am plunged by the power of the devil, and I was ignorant of your Holy Name; I walked among the sheep, and they left me at once, and the clouds could not give rain on the Earth, which was dry and barren, nor the trees bear fruit and the women were barren; I closed the passages of the Sea, and it was impossible to open them. I myself did all these evils, and an infinite number of others. But now, my Lord Jesus Christ and my God, since I know and love your Holy Name, I repent with all my heart, with all my soul and with all my entrails of the multitude of my mischiefs, iniquities and crimes, and now form the resolution to abide in your love and submit to your holy commandment, because you are the one and only Word of the Almighty Father.

I beseech you now, my God, to break the bonds of the clouds, to loosen them, to cause them to fall upon the Earth and upon your children gentle, sweet and favourable rains, which will produce their food as well as that of all the animals that live in the waters, by loosening the rivers that I had bound as well as all the rest; I beseech you by your most Holy Name; and you, my God, preserve me N. who am your creature, from all danger † and from all evil † I beseech you by your Holy Name to whom all things, both spiritual and corporeal, owe honour and glory. And by Emmanuel, which means God be in us; and say to the waters, I have sanctified the gates and places through which you pass: and you have delivered, Lord, the children of Israel from the captivity of Pharaoh: deign also to deliver me from all evils, perils and dangers.

I beseech you, I, N., who has the joy of being your creature, through your servants Moses and Aaron; extend over me N. your right hand to pour your holy blessing on me N.; you are my God, bless me as you have blessed your good Angels, that is, your Angels, Archangels, Thrones, Dominations, Principalities, Powers, Virtues, Cherubim, Seraphim. Deign also to bless me N., my Lord Jesus Christ; bless me, your creature, in such a way that no foul spirit or demon can harm me, that I may not be stained, that their evil deeds and evil intentions, nor the malignity of their eyes, nor their poisonous tongues, nor any persecution on their part, may have any effect on me.

Remove from us, Lord, all evil, all malignant spirits, may all evil men and pernicious women distance themselves from us, flee us, and we from them, may all our enemies and adversaries distance themselves from us, may they have no influence or power over us, we ask you by the virtue of the Most High, and if anyone, Lord, wants to harm me and do the least evil, put me under your holy protection, my God, I, N., who am your creature, and deign to do me every good; I ask you by the virtue and merits of your holy Angels, who being God, praise you unceasingly, and by all your patriarchs, your apostles, saints of Paradise, to deliver and preserve your servant from the malignity of the eyes of all my enemies and even those who could harm me. So be it.

I beg you again, my Lord Jesus Christ, by all the holy prayers that are generally said in all the churches of Christendom, to set me free and deliver me from the malignity of all evil deeds, from all the evil that can be done by all demons, evil men and evil women; I beg you by the name of the Cherubim and Seraphim, that they have no power or reach over us.

I beseech you most humbly, God the Father, most gentle and most merciful, by your Annunciation, by your Death and burial, by your wonderful and marvellous Ascension, by the coming and arrival of the Holy Spirit on Earth, and by the prayers of all the saints, by the contrition of all holy pilgrims, by the beauty of Adam, by the sacrifice of Abel, by the deliverance of Noah, by the faith of Abraham, by the offering of Isaac, by the religion of Melchisedech, by the humility of Job, by the holy love of Moses, by the sacrifice of Abraham, by the religion of Aaron and the psalms of David, by the annunciation of Isaac, by the tears of Jeremiah, by the contrition of Zechariah, by the depth of the abyss of Hell, by the height of Heaven, by the clarity of the Divinity, by the tongues of the apostles, by the ways of

P III

the evangelists and Angels, by the one who saw Moses, by the brightness of the lights, by the holy discourses and preaching of the apostles, by the baptism of Our Lord Jesus Christ, by the voice of the Heavenly Father who said from his throne and was heard on Earth. This is my beloved Son, in whom I have placed all my kindness, listen to what he tells you; and by the miracle when Jesus Christ fed five thousand people in the desert with five fish and two loaves of bread, by the miracle he performed when he resurrected Lazarus from the dead, and by all those who fear God. I beseech you, Lord, to break all these bonds, and preserve me from the charm of their eyes, me N., who am the servant of God.

I beseech you, Lord, by all these holy deeds, and by all the virtues which are written in this Book to the praise and honour of the great living God, for not having harmed me N. who am your servant, may this great

God, I say, who created all things, not allow any of their magic, spells or curses, if they have used them, to have any power over gold, silver, brass, iron, or anything that is worked or chiselled, or rough, or on silks, or wools, or on linens and cloths made of all these materials, on generally all bones, both of men and women, fish, wood or anything else, or on herbs, or on any books or papers or blank parchments; if they have put it or caused it to be put on any stone, in water, wine, bread, cheese, or in the Earth or on the Earth, or in the sepulchre of any giant, or Hebrew, or pagan, or Christian, or in or upon the hair, clothes, shoes, any fastener or strap, and in a word, in or on anything whatsoever, that is to say in whatever place or thing all these evil deeds are done or must be done.

I most humbly ask and beseech you by the virtue of God the Father most powerful, and of the Son, and of the Holy Spirit, to destroy them and render them without effect and that they have no power over me † N. who am your servant. I beg you through the merits of Saint Cyprian.

Do, O my God, my sovereign, that I, N.,
who am your creature, may be delivered from every evil deed, every peril, every
mischief, from the pernicious tongue and
eye of my enemies who seek to harm and
destroy me. O God the Almighty and eternal Father, deliver me from all the dangers
that surround me, as you delivered the three
children, Sidrac, Misaac and Abdenago, from
the furnace of fire; also deliver your servant
from all peril and danger, both of body and
soul.

Here are the Names of Jesus Christ; whoever carries them with him on his journey, both on Land and Sea, will be preserved from all kinds of dangers and perils, when said with faith and devotion.

TRINITY † Agios † Sother † Messiah † Emmanuel † Sabaoth and Adonay † Athanatos † Jesus † Pentagna † Agiagon † Ischiros † Eleïson † O Theos † Tetragrammaton † Ely † Saday † Eagle † Great Man † Sight † Flower † Source † Saviour † Alpha † & Omega † First Born † Wisdom † Virtue † Comforter † Way † Truth † and Life † Mediator † Physician † Salvation † Lamb † Sheep † Calf † Hope † Ram † Lion † Worm † Mouth † Word † or Verb † Splendour † Sun † Glory † Light † Image † Bread † Gate † Stone † Bride † Shepherd † Prophet † Priest † Holy † Immortal † Jesus Christ † Father † Son †

Holy Man † God † Agios † Resurrection †
Mischios † Charity † Eternity † Creator †
Redeemer † Unity † Sovereign Good † Evam
†.

Here are the Names of the Blessed Virgin.

L IFE † Virgin † Flower † Cloud † Queen
† Theotokos † All † Silent † Empress †
Pacific † Mistress † Earth † Birth † Fountain †
Well † Path † Woman † Dawn † Moon † Sun †
Door † House † Temple † Blessed † Glorious
† Pious † Court † Principle † End † School
† Ladder † Star fervent † Cluster † Vine †
Tower † Vessel † Redemptress † Liberator
† Ark † Bed † Cinnamon † Generation †
Woman † Friend † Valley † Vallon † Trumpet
† Thorn † † Beautiful Stone † Mother † Alana
† Well-made † Rose † Blessed Door † Libur
† City † Dove † Pomegranate † Tabernacle †
Great † Mary. † So be it. † So be it. †

In honour of God and the blessed Saint Cyprian. Let us give thanks to God. So be it.

Orison to Saint Michael for those who travel on water; also used against sheep pox.

ARCHANGEL Michael, who has custody of Paradise, come and help the people of God, and be pleased to defend us against the Demon, and generally from all our enemies who are very powerful, and lead us into the presence of God in the abode of the blessed.

℣. Lord, my God, I will sing your praises in the presence of your Angels.

℟. I will pay you my most humble homage in your holy Temple, and I will publish the greatness of your Name.

This figure is the measurement of the wound on the side of Jesus Christ. Whoever wears it on oneself must not fear any pitfalls of his enemies, both visible and invisible, and any pregnant woman in labour from childbirth will have prompt help, provided only that she sees it. It gives victory over enemies, guarantees from any loss, damage and sudden death.

To exorcise it, one needs virgin parchment, as well as the other instruments, and this on Holy Friday, at one hour past midnight, having first recited the whole Passion, after which one will make the aforementioned figure, perfume it with good odours, then wear it on oneself.

Recommandation.

Recommendation to the four Evangelists,
before retiring to bed:

† *Huic thalamo præsto lucas defensor adesto.*

† *Marce precare Jesum ne simus Dæmonis œsu.*

† *Te precor ut damnes fantasmata cuncta Joannes.*

† *Esto custos meus dum dormiam nocte Mattheus.*

† *Jesu Filii David miserere mei. Amen.*

† *In nomme Patris † et Filii, † et Spiritus sancti.
† Amen.*

*Orison of Pope Leo, to remove
all spells and enchantments.*

AGAROTH, † Aphonidos, † Paatia † Urat, Condion, † Lamacron, † Fondon, † Arpagon, † Alamar, † Bourgasis *veniat* Serebani.

Mystical Secrets to charm weapons.

De valanda jacem mafix darafia excorbis.

Mystical Secret to guard sheep.

WRITE on virgin parchment on Holy Friday during the Passion, Otheos, † Ortoo, † Noxio, † Bay, † Gloy, † Apenib, † then put this writing in the handle of the crook, and planting it upright, the sheep will not stray from it.

To cure swollen sheep.

GOT *et magot et super magot et consummatum est.* Make the sign of the Cross with your left foot, pronouncing the above words as you enter the pasture, they will be preserved. And to heal them if they are swollen,

P. 121
G
✠ ANANIZAPTA
✠ ✠ JOHAZATH
I ✠ A

you should repeat them three times on each animal, making them stand upright without agitation.

Against sheep scab.

TAKE two or three strands of linen, wrap them around a small boxwood stick, dip it and pass it through the animal's foundation three times in succession, saying: *passe fratres nobis.*

Key and Mysterious Table of the Orisons and Secrets contained in this Book.

THE two Pentacles, one of which is on the frontispiece and the other at the end of this Book, have a powerful virtue to bind and hold in check the most resolute spirits; it is their sentence and their condemnation: as soon as you show them, they have no difficulty in obeying you in all things. It should be noted that no strong and powerful magic book can be made without these two Pentacles imprinted on it. They must be made on virgin goat parchment, exorcised and blessed, and a Mass of the Holy Spirit must be said over them, after which the Pentacles will be made on Wednesday night, at the hour of Mercury.

Nota.—That one must have exorcised his ink and pen, which will have never been used. It is necessary to be chaste, and alone in a solitary place, and to be pure and clean for three days, both from the inside and the outside; the same conduct must be observed in all other operations.

After making the circle, it will be blessed, sprinkling holy water on it, saying: *Asparagus mes, etc...* After the Pentacles have been made, they should be perfumed with odoriferous scents, then placed in a clean earthen vase, where they should remain for three days and

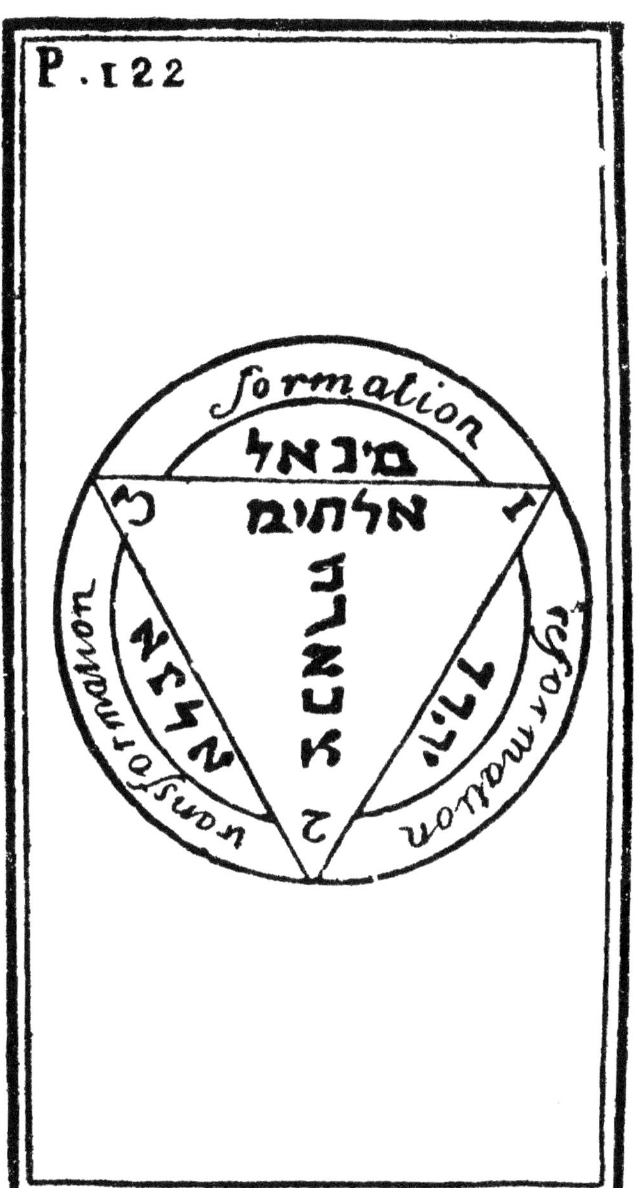
formation
reformation
transformation
3
1
2
מנאל
אלהים
אלעאר
יהוה
אלשא

three nights ; they should then be placed in a pure, white cloth, to preserve them preciously, lest they be profaned, until they are placed in some book, to which being attached, the book should be incensed and exorcised, and placed in a pure place, to be opened only when necessary.

Prayer before any operation.

Almighty God, God most strong, God most gentle, God most high and most glorious, God sovereign and fair, O God full of all grace and mercy, I throw myself at your feet, I, N., who am an unworthy sinner. I come before your Majesty, I implore your mercy and your goodness, do not look at the infinite multitude of my sins, since you always have compassion on penitents, deign to hear my prayers ; bless, I beg you, my operation by your goodness, your mercy and your

almighty virtue. This is the grace I ask of you
† in the name of your Son, † who reigns with
you and the Holy Spirit, † for ever and ever.
So be it. Then say the Dominical Orison five
times, and the Angelic Salutation.

Exorcisms of parchment, ink and quill.

I EXORCISE you, foul spirit, spirit of delusion,
so that in the Name of the Almighty God
you need to depart from this operation, and
that all your malice being removed from us,
these things we exorcise remain sanctified.
In the name of the Father, † of the Son, †
and of the Holy Spirit. † So be it. That I, N.,
by the virtue of these perfumes, may be sus-
tained by all the virtue of the spirit of God
and that no delusion may harm me, which
I thereby ask by the great and formidable
Name of God Samhammaphoras.

Blessing of perfume.

GOD of Abraham, † God of Isaac, † God of Jacob, † bless this creature N., that it may redouble the strength and virtue of its odours, so that it may contain the spirits which I must evoke by the perfection of my work and my desire; I ask this through your Son Our Lord Jesus, who lives and reigns with you in the unity of the Holy Spirit, through all the centuries of ages. So be it.

Exorcism of Fire.

HAVING placed it in a new earthen vessel, say over it: I exorcise you, creature of fire, by him who made and created all things, so that all phantoms that might harm me may depart from you.

Blessing of Fire.

G OD of Abraham † God of Isaac † God of Jacob † bless this creature N., so that being blessed and sanctified in honour of your Holy Name, it may keep away from all those who will wear it or see phantoms or harmful enemies; this we ask of you through your only Son Our Saviour Jesus Christ, who lives and reigns, etc...

Virtues of the Seven Psalms,
taken from the Cabala, page 6.

The Gospel according to Saint John, page 5.

Is intended to protect against all accidents during the day, being said in the morning when getting up, having sprinkled oneself in the face with holy water, saying: *Asperges mes, etc.* Next, stand against the wall to avoid being seen by anyone, strike the chest three times, saying: *Confiteor, etc.*, then stand up and recite the said Gospel. Remain in your room for another half-hour, reciting the *seven Psalms,* the *Litany of the Saints* and the *Pater noster.*

If one carries the aforementioned Gospel, written on virgin parchment and enclosed in a Goose feather pipe, on the first Sunday of the year, one hour before sunrise, one will be invulnerable and protected against many evils.

Against all kinds of charms, etc.
page 20.

Seven mysterious Orisons for each day of the week, intended in general against all kinds of dangers, evils, misfortunes and accidents, *page 26* and those that follow.

To use these seven Orisons, it is necessary, on the first Tuesday of the Moon before sunrise, give alms to the first poor you find in the Church, where you will hear a mass. Then, when you have returned, write the afore-mentioned Orisons on virgin parchment; the crosses you find there must be marked with blood drawn from the middle finger of your left hand and, for each cross you draw, you must make one on yourself; after that, bless and incense the aforementioned Orisons and, carrying them with you, you will be pre-served from all kinds of ambushes from your enemies.

Against the adversities of the world, page 41.

The Orison, *He will break the bow, etc.*, must be accompanied by that of the Virgin, *page 41,* and that which begins with *The right hand of the Lord, etc., page 42.*

These three Orisons are to be written on Monday at midnight, having only for light a yellow wax candle on the table; before writ-ing them, say the following:

You will walk boldly over the asp and the basilisk, you will crumple the head of the Lion and the Dragon.

Then write with boldness these Orisons on virgin parchment made of exorcised Deer and, carrying them with you, you can tame, overcome and destroy your enemies ; the first of these Orisons is used to charm weapons.

Orison of great virtue, page 43.

To use this Orison, it must be written on virgin parchment on the first Monday of the Moon, before sunrise. The parchment must have been exorcised and three Masses of the Holy Spirit said on it on three different Mondays. Then, go and gather Vervain on a Friday, at the hour of Venus ; when you are near the said herb, extend your left hand on it, having the face turned toward the East, then say : *facta isquina fatos joara, herb whose virtue is admirable and produces marvellous effects, I pick you so that you may serve me as I wish.* Pliny, the naturalist, says that magicians claim that this herb must be picked toward the beginning of a canicular day, when the Sun and Moon are not on the earth, having previously buried honeycombs and honey to satisfy and soothe the earth, after it has been loosened with an iron pick, it must be picked with the left hand and not allowed to fall to the ground; the leaves, stem and root are dried separately in the shade. Carrying this herb with you in the manner we have just taught, you will obtain everything you can ask for, and you will not be refused a girl in marriage, however rich she may be; but you must refrain from swearing or going to any place of debauchery when you carry this herb, as it will become unfruitful. In addition, you must say the aforementioned Orison every morning before sunrise, with a *Pater* and *Ave.*

This Orison is used to see in a dream what one wishes. When one feels succumbing or being weak about anything, one recites the said Orison and the one that follows, making as many signs of the cross as there are when writing it; they are to be written on the first Friday of the Moon, one hour before sunrise; the crosses must be marked with blood drawn from the thumb of the left hand, all on virgin parchment.

When you want to perform the experiment, put these Orisons under the pillow of the bed, on the side of the ear you usually sleep; the best is to put them on near the left ear and you will see the effect of what you desire.

Orison: O Lord Jesus Christ,
page 53.

To use this Orison, it should be written on Tuesday, at eleven in the evening; the crosses should be traced with blood drawn from the finger following the thumb of the left hand; it is used to identify accomplices in a crime or theft.

Nota.—It must be written on virgin parchment, and one must not eat or drink for seven hours. The next day, Wednesday, you must not eat or drink until the Sun has set, and having done so, you must put it under your head as you go to bed; you will know by experiment the effect of your request. It is also useful against one's enemies, adding the one before which begins: *Now, Jesus passing in the midst of them, etc., page 50.*

It is necessary to write it three times, on virgin parchment, before departure, before sunrise, reciting Psalm 125 beforehand: *In convertendo*; The crosses will be formed from blood drawn from the little finger of the left hand; two of these crosses will be traced with blessed charcoal from the left hand; then Psalm 58 will be recited: *Deus, in nomine tuo salvum me fac.* Carrying this Orison with you, you will be feared and dreaded by your enemies, being magicians, evil spirits, thieves or others, and you will obtain the requests you make when travelling; you will frighten all those who wish you wrong.

Exhorting to Jesus Christ
Hagios, page 58.

You shall write these holy names on virgin parchment on any day before sunrise, and make the crosses from your own blood drawn from the little finger of your left hand, then incense and perfume it and carry it with you, with veneration, and you shall be preserved from all danger.

To make a woman faithful
O good Jesus, etc., page 64.

We begin to write the crosses of this Orison on common paper with ordinary ink; we then trace them with the left hand on virgin parchment, also for *Adonay Job Magister dicit Jo* with blessed coal, and this on the first Monday of the Moon at its hour. The crosses on the paper are then thrown into the fire, saying: "May you burn forever and not come with me to judgment." Afterwards, you will carry the parchment with you; then the Orison will be written on red paper. On Tuesday, in the hour of Mars, crosses will be made with unused black ink, into which three drops of blood from the middle finger of the right hand will be poured. Wearing this Orison, the woman will be faithful unto death.

The great Saint Leo, Pope, etc...
page 81.

One must write this Orison on Sunday at the hour of the Sun on virgin parchment, first making the sign of the cross, and all those found will be marked with the blood of the left little finger, making as many signs of the cross over oneself ; Psalm 50 is to be recited. Carrying this parchment on oneself, one will obtain what he wishes from the great and princes.

Orison, I entreat you, Peter, etc...
page 87.

Used to be invincible, glorious in battle, in the siege of a city and in forcing an enemy camp. This Orison and the other two that follow being written on virgin parchment on Thursday at eleven in the evening; the crosses must be made with Sanguine without making the sign of the cross. Before anything else, say the Psalm *Judica, Deus, nocentes*, and the Orison *Obsecro te, Deus*. Do not omit the Numbers and Characters, which are the supputation of the Demon of Jupiter, who rules over the planet Venus. The characters L. M. are the names of *Limoch* and *Machel*, of which one governs the winds of the earth and the other stops lightning and storms. By these Characters, hidden treasures can be raised without noise, placing them on the spot at the hour as above (all things being observed as we have indicated). We carry the said parchment, between midnight and one hour, between three paths where we will make a circle and a hole in the middle, then the parchment being wrapped in a clean cloth, will be put in the ground and covered with a new earthen dish, then we recite the aforementioned Orisons, and those which are under the dish will serve to conjure the spirits and prevent their impetuosity, and keep them under control. If this experiment is carried out on Holy Saturday, it will be more certain; the crosses will be marked with common charcoal; they will be removed three days later at the same time, and will be useful for whatever you wish.

Against arrows, etc., page 88.

Orisons against all charms and poisons, etc., page 91.

Barnasa, etc. This Orison is to be written on paper soaked in the blood of a Goat, having dried it on a Wednesday, at the hour of Mercury. The first cross is to be made with the left hand, all the rest with the right hand, with an unused pen and ink, into which three drops of the Goat's blood have been mixed. Having finished, make three signs of the cross, recite Psalm 44; then carry the Orison with you, and do not be afraid, for marble will not be harder than you.

To use this Orison, you must fast three days before writing it, and on the fourth day before sunrise, having prayed to God, say Psalm 50; write it on blessed virgin parchment, then incense it with good perfume, then wrap it in blessed white satin and carry it with you.

This Orison is of great virtue in making oneself loved and bringing in the person one wishes. Before writing it, you must fast for three days and have three masses said and intended for the most neglected soul; every time you leave your home to have the mass said, you must give alms to the first poor to come by; then, on the first Friday of the Moon, at six in the morning, you recite the Psalm *Principes, the princes persecuted, etc...* Then the Orison is written on virgin parchment with a pen and ink that have never been used; when it is written, the Psalm *Magnificat* is to be recited standing straight; then the Orison is incensed and carried on oneself. When you want to make a person come to you, recite the aforementioned Orison three times on that day, after which, say: "Let (name the person's name and nickname) come here as soon as possible."

To use this Orison, recite it three times on the first Thursday of the crescent of the Moon, before sunrise, and three more times before sunset, at the hour of Jupiter ; and the next day, Friday, at the hour of Venus, write it on exorcised white paper, with new ink and pen ; after which, recite Psalm 118, *Immaculati omnes, etc...*, Then perfume it and carry it with you. Above the said Orison, write : *Valeam da Zarac.* † Which having done, it will serve to enter into grace with princes and great lords, hosts and relatives.

That these holy names, etc... It is the Orison of Holy Alosee, etc... Pathay. This Orison must be written on paper on Friday at eleven in the evening, having said, prior to this, *these holy names, etc.,* you will soon see your enemies come to pay you homage, etc., *page 101.*

Before writing it, fast for three days and confess, then recite the following: "O Lord, enlighten me on this day when I write the sentence of the demons; purify me, O my God, who live and reign for ever and ever. So be it." It is written on virgin parchment on a Sunday at sunrise, then incensed and wrapped in a fine, clean cloth; once this is done, when you want to see the effect, fast and confess as above. It is of great to evoke and bind demons.

This Orison is written on virgin parchment on any day before sunrise; the crosses are marked with blood drawn from the little finger of the left hand, then incensed and carried on the person.

Here are the names of the Blessed Virgin,
page 116.

This Orison is written on virgin parchment; the crosses are made of blood drawn from the ring finger of the left hand on any day before sunrise; incense it, recite the entire Office of the Conception and carry it with you. It is used to obtain graces from the Blessed Virgin.

Orison of Holy Michael, page 117.

It is used against sheep pox, for those who travel on water, to be preserved from snares, temptations and the bites of poisonous beasts. Written on virgin parchment on the day of the Feast of Saint Michael before sunrise, it is incensed and carried in honour of God and Saint Cyprian.

Figure of the wound on the side of Jesus Christ and its virtues, page 118.

Recommendation to the four Evangelists, etc. page 119.

On the day of the feast of each evangelist, you shall say a mass; you shall write the said Orison on the day of the first mass before sunrise, on virgin parchment; the crosses shall be marked with blood drawn from the four fingers of the left hand; after which, you shall incense and perfume it, and wear it on your person. It is used to win at gambling, traffic, trade or commerce.

MYSTICAL SECRETS.

Conjuration for the spirits of Air, to the Angels governing the Air that day and having implored their help in this way, one after the other.

I CONJURE and beg you to be favourable to me, and to listen to the requests I wish to make of you, and to come promptly to my aid, and to help me and lead to a happy success the operation I am now beginning, and I shall be obliged to you.

This finished, he will say: I conjure you, O Angels, all as many as you are (naming them each by their names) and compel you by the seat of the great God, Adonay, Agios, O Theos, Ischyros, Athanatos, Paraclytus, Alpha & Omega, and by the three Sacred Names of God, Agla, On, Tetragrammaton, that you have to accomplish today what I desire.

You will say the conjuration of the specific day which you will find in the Grimoire of Pope Honorius, after having done the above.

If the spirits, after the appropriate conjuration on the assigned day, remain obstinate, not heeding the Orisons or commands made to them on behalf of the great living God, the master of the operation will make and recite the following exorcism, which is such:

Orison.

AMERULA, Tancha, Latiston, Zabac, Jancha, Escha, Aladia, Alpha & Omega, Leiste, Oriston, Adonay, my heavenly Father, most merciful, have mercy on me, miserable sinner that I am; extend today the arm of your omnipotence over me and strengthen me against the obstinate spirits, so that in consideration of your divine greatness, I may be endowed with all wisdom, to praise and glorify your Holy Name. I therefore beseech you, my Lord and my God, and invoke you from the bottom of my heart, so that, by your irrevocable judgment, the spirits I call may be obliged to come and bring to me whenever I call them and give me a true answer to what I ask of them, without any harm to any creature of my company, nor any other whatsoever, without causing wrong either to my life, or to my spirits, or to my senses of nature, and thus leaving me full liberty of my five senses of nature, and to my companions, without causing me horror or fear of any kind, without noise and without scandal, they come to answer me truthfully to whatever I shall ask them. Through you, my Creator and my God, who lives and reigns forever.

Licence to depart.

I CONJURE you, Spirit N., such as you are, to leave me in peace and rest, and go to the abode God has destined for you for all eternity. Through Our Lord Jesus Christ, who lives and reigns forever and ever. *Amen.* I licence you to depart and may you appear to me whenever and wherever I call you, by the mere words of your name, striking three times against the ground, to carry out my will and desire.

L ITTLE white Paternoster that God made, that God said, that God put in Paradise. In the evening, when I went to bed, I found three Angels lying by my bed, one at my feet, two at my bedside, the good Virgin Mary in the middle who told me that I was lying down, that nothing should be doubted. The Good Lord is my Father, the Blessed Virgin my Mother, the three apostles my brothers, the three virgins my sisters. The shirt where God was born, my body is wrapped in it, the Cross of Saint Marguerite to my chest is written; Madame goes on the fields to God weeping, met Mr. Saint John. "Mr. Saint John, where are you from?" "I come from *Ave Salus.*" "You have not seen the Good Lord: if then, he is in the tree of the Cross, his feet dangling, his hands nailing, a little hat of white thorn on his head." Whoever says it three times in the morning will earn Paradise in the end.

MYSTICAL SECRETS

To stop the course of a fire, burning a house.

S AY : Let it stop, let it stop. I hoped before you, Lord, who confound your glory in eternity.

Otherwise.

M AKE three crosses on the mantelpiece with a charcoal and write : *In te, Domine speravi, non confundar in æternum.*

To be protected against firearms.

S AY thrice : God is part of it and Notre-Dame. I see the muzzle of the musket, God guards the entrance and the Devil the exit.

For love.

T AKE a four-leaf Clover and put it on the blessed stone; let a mass be said over it, then put it in a bouquet and let the person you wish to be loved smell it, saying: *Gabriel illa sunt.*

To cure colic.

P UT your large finger on your navel and say: Marri qui est mari, or colic passion which is between my liver and my heart, between my spleen and my lung: I stop you in the name of the Father † and of the Son † and of the Holy Spirit †. And say three *Pater* and *Ave*, and name the patient, saying: God has healed you.

To stop a carriage or cart.

I T is necessary to place a small stick in the middle of the road, on which are written the words : *Jerusalem omnipotens Deus, convert thy-self there*; then cross the road through which the carriage or cart is to pass.

To win at games.

G ATHER fern on Saint John's eve, at noon; make a bracelet from it in the shape of these characters, HUTY.

Walking garter which protects against
all perils and dangers.

T AKE some Scarlet, make a garter that can surround your hock and, on it, put nine hairs from a hanged person; then, buy some white satin of the same length, on which you will write with your blood: *verbum caro factum est et habitavit in nobis.* Put the satin on the Scarlet and let the words touch the hair. Put the garter on your left hock, the satin against the flesh: as soon as you arrive, remove the garter, to use it again when necessary; have your bed washed in sugar and wash the soles of your feet with wine.

*To prevent a hunter from shooting
and kill anything.*

S AY: *Si ergo me quæretis, finite.*

To draw the white ticket at the militia.

S AY: Lord, who did not wish your robe to be torn, but was thrown to fate, do me the grace, I, who draw today, that I be

exempt; Lord, exempt me; Lord, exempt
me; Lord, exempt me, please; then say three
times *Pater*, etc...

To put peace between people who are fighting.

WRITE around an apple: HAON, and
throw it into the midst of the com-
batants.

To stop blood.

SAY: Place ††† *consummatum* †††
resurrexit ††† on the spot.

To heal a burn.

SAY three times over the burn, each time
blowing your breath over it: Fire of
God, lose your heat as Judas lost his colour,

when he betrayed Our Lord in the Garden
of Olives.

To punish the insolent.

O N a Saturday morning, before sunrise,
cut a one year old branch of Hazel,
saying: I cut you, branch of this summer, in
the name which I have the intent to mutilate.
Then put a blanket over the table, saying:
† *In nomine Paris* † *et Filii* † *et Spiritus Sancti.*
Say this three times with the following: *Et
in Cute* Drock † Mirroch † Esenaroth † Betu
† Baroc † Maaroth; then say: Holy Trinity,
punish the one who has done me this evil
and remove it by your great justice † Eson †
Elion † Esmaris, and, at the last words, strike
the blanket, and the person concerned will
receive the same blows. It is understood, by
blanket, a garment or carpet, etc... Note that
if you cut a branch from the said Hazel tree,

with the intention of mutilating the limb of someone, you must say so as you cut it, and when you wish to heal the person, cut another branch from the said tree with this intention, and you will strike it as above, and he will infallibly heal. When you want to do the same to another person, you will only say: Holy Trinity, punish N. † Eson † Elion † Esmaris; with the words of these Angels, strike as above with the suitable rod, and notice that these two rods serve forever; but no branches must have been cut beforehand from this Hazel tree.

*To stop hail and storms
caused by evil spells.*

MAKE the sign of the cross against flashes, hail, lightning and storms, then take three stones of hail from the first fall, and throw them into the fire in the name of the adorable Trinity and, having said the Sunday Orison two or three times, recite the Gospel of Saint John, which when completed, you need to make the sign of the cross against the cloud and thunder on all sides, and again mark the same salutary sign on the Earth, toward the four parts of the world; then, having said *verbum caro factum est,* three times, add as many times: *per Evangelica dicta fugiat tempestas ista.*

To heal ulcers.

FIRST prepare the compress, making two pieces and placing them to form a cross, on which you will recite the following words three times:

God was born on Christmas night.
God died.
God rose from the dead.
God commanded the wounds to be closed.

That the pain stops

That the blood stops.

And it does not enter into matter or scent, as did the five wounds of Our Saviour, Jesus Christ. *In nomine Paris, † et Filii, † et Spiritus Sancti, † Amen.*

This done, carry it to the table, then suck on the wound three times, then take oil and say three times over it:

Natus est Christus †

Mortuus est Christus †

Resurrexit Christus †

Then, place it in the mouth and blow it into the wound, and apply the compress and, if the wound has come out, do the same there again.

To lift all spells and enchantments.

TAKE the heart of a Sheep and pierce it with nails, and hang it over the chimney, saying: Rostin Clasta, Auvara, Chasta, Custodia, Duranée. You must say these same words over the heart; and the eighth day will not pass until the sorcerer who cast the spell comes to beg you to leave the heart, because he feels great pain in his chest. Then you will ask him to remove the spell, and he will ask you for some animal to cast it on him, which you can grant him; otherwise he will die through the middle of his body.

To discover thieves.

WRITE separately on pieces of paper all the names of those who are in the house, masters, valets and others. Throw the papers into a brazen pan full of clear water; then say over them: I conjure you, Onazarde, Arogani, Labilafs, Parandomo, Azigola, Maractatam, Siranday, Eptaleton, Lamboured, to let me know the thief. Then, if his name is in the pan it will rise to the surface, and if two or more come, they are accomplices.

Against hemorrhoids.

THEY need to be pushed back three times with the middle finger of the right hand, each time saying: Broka broket, which God made for me; I no longer have them through Jesus. In the name of the Father, and of the Son, and of the Holy Spirit. So be it.

Against the flow of blood.

SAY: *Anna peririt Mariam, Elizabeth peririt Joannem. Maria autem Christum. In nomine Jesu cesset sanguis ab hoc famulo, vel ab hac famula.*

For a pricked or nailed horse.

SAY: *Pater noster, etc.,* to *in cælo, et in terra, etc. In nomine, etc. Amen.* In honour of God and of Mr. Saint Eloy.

For the canker that befalls woollen animals.

WHITE canker, black canker, red canker, canker of all kinds, I conjure you to have no more hold on this herd, than the Devil has on the Priest, when he says the Holy Mass.

Against sickness and wounds.

I KNOW a village sergeant who says the following Orison for all the sick and wounded who come to him, and who request him to say it. In the name of the Father, and of the Son, and of the Holy Spirit. Madam Saint Anne who gave birth to the Virgin Mary, the Virgin Mary who gave birth to Jesus Christ, God bless you and heal you, poor creature N., from relapsing, broking and blocking, and from all kinds of wounds whatsoever, in honour of God, and of the Virgin Mary, Gentlemen Saint Côme and Saint Damien, Amen. Then three *Pater* and *Ave.* And what is considerable, is that this Orison, all eloquent and all spiritual as it is, heals almost all those for whom it is said, as several people worthy of faith have assured.

For eye sickness.

MR. Saint Jean was passing by and saw three Virgins on his way, and said to them : What are you doing here ? We are healing mesh. O heal, virgins, heal the eye of N. making the sign of the cross and blowing into the eye, he continues : mesh, fire of grievances, fire of whatsoever, nails, migraine and spider, I command you to have no more power over this eye than the Jews had on Passover day over the body of Our Lord Jesus Christ. Then again, make the sign of the cross and blow into the eye of the sick, ordering him to say three *Pater* and three *Ave*. In the name of the Father, and of the Son, and of the Holy Spirit.

Against toothache.

WRITE these words and hang them around the neck: *Stragiles falcesque dentate dentium dolorem persanate.*

Divination by the sieve.

WHEN you are determined to know something secret, you place the sieve between the two points of a pair of shearing forces, then two people each put the middle finger of their left hand under the handle of the forces where the sieve is attached, and hold it up in the air, then pronounce what you want to know, saying: O sieve, you will turn, if it is so-and-so who has such and such a thing; then pronounce the mysterious words: Dies Mies Jeschet, Benedœdet, Dowima Enitemaü. If the person named is guilty, the sieve will shake, turn and fall; if not, start again with another name.

For a burn.

Our Holy Father goes down his way, finds a child who cries out: Father, what's wrong with this child? He is burned to a crisp. Take some Pig's breast, and three *fascines* of your body, and the fire will go out.

For epilepsy.

B LOW these words into the right ear of the one who has fallen: *Gaspar fert myrr-ham, thus Melchior, Baltazar aurum.* He will rise immediately. And to heal him radically, you must have three iron nails, the length of his little finger, drive them deep into the place where he first fell, and on each one name the patient.

Against the Foxes.

S AY three times a week: In the name of the Father, † and of the Son, † and of the Holy Spirit † Foxes, I conjure you, in the name of the most holy and blessed, as Our Lady was with child, that you neither take nor discard any of my birds, from my flock, either Roosters, Hens or Chickens, nor eat their nests, nor suck their blood, nor break their eggs, nor do them any harm, etc.

Against Wolves.

R ECITE the same Orison and say, instead of Foxes, the name of the beats you wish to preserve from Wolves.

To be hard.

W RITE on two pieces of paper with your blood the following: Ranuc † Malin † *Fora consummatum est, in te confedo, Satana,* † you will swallow one and wear the other around your neck.

END

SUPPLEMENT

THE PSALMS

Supplement material to the 1660 edition, to conjure the Intelligences by means of the Psalms described in the first part of this Book, both in Latin and English.

Psalm 6.

2 Domine, ne in furore tuo arguas me, neque in ira tua corripias me. 3 Miserere mei, Domine, quoniam infirmus sum; sana me, Domine, quoniam conturbata sunt ossa mea. 4 Et anima mea turbata est valde; sed tu, Domine, usquequo? 5 Convertere, Domine, et eripe animam meam; salvum me fac propter misericordiam tuam. 6 Quoniam non est in morte qui memor sit tui; in inferno autem quis confitebitur tibi? 7 Laboravi in gemitu meo; lavabo per singulas noctes lectum meum: lacrimis meis stratum meum rigabo. 8 Turbatus est a furore oculus meus; inveteravi inter omnes inimicos meos. 9 Discedite a me omnes qui operamini iniquitatem, quoniam exaudivit Dominus vocem fletus mei. 10 Exaudivit Dominus deprecationem meam; Dominus orationem meam suscepit. 11 Erubescant, et conturbentur vehementer, omnes inimici mei; convertantur, et erubescant valde velociter.

2 Lord, when thou dost reprove me, let it not be in anger; when thou dost chastise me, let it not be in displeasure. 3 Lord, pity me; I have no strength left; Lord, heal me; my limbs tremble; 4 my spirits are altogether broken; Lord, wilt thou never be content? 5 Lord, turn back, and grant a wretched soul relief; as thou art ever merciful, save me. 6 When death comes, there is no more remembering thee; none can praise thee in the tomb. 7 I am spent with sighing; every night I lie weeping on my bed, till the tears drench my pillow. 8 Grief has dimmed my eyes, faded their lustre now, so many are the adversaries that surround me. 9 Depart from me, all you that traffic in iniquity; the Lord has heard my cry of distress. 10 Here was a prayer divinely heard, a boon divinely granted. 11 All my enemies will be abashed and terrified; taken aback, all in a moment, and put to shame.

Psalm 31.

1 Beati quorum remissæ sunt iniquitates, et quorum tecta sunt peccata. 2 Beatus vir cui non imputavit Dominus peccatum, nec est in spiritu ejus dolus. 3 Quoniam tacui, inveteraverunt ossa mea, dum clamarem tota die. 4 Quoniam die ac nocte gravata est super me manus tua, conversus sum in ærumna mea, dum configitur spina. 5 Delictum meum cognitum tibi feci, et injustitiam meam non abscondi. Dixi: Confitebor adversum me injustitiam meam Domino; et tu remisisti impietatem peccati mei. 6 Pro hac orabit ad te omnis sanctus in tempore opportuno. Verumtamen in diluvio aquarum multarum, ad eum non approximabunt. 7 Tu es refugium meum a tribulatione quæ circumdedit me; exsultatio mea, erue me a circumdantibus me. 8 Intellectum tibi dabo, et instruam te in via hac qua gradieris; firmabo super te oculos meos. 9 Nolite fieri sicut equus et mulus, quibus non est intellectus. In camo et freno maxillas eorum constringe, qui

non approximant ad te. 10 Multa flagella pecca-
toris; sperantem autem in Domino misericordia
circumdabit. 11 Lætamini in Domino, et exsul-
tate, justi; et gloriamini, omnes recti corde.

1 Blessed are they who have their faults forgiven, their transgressions buried deep; 2 blessed
is the man who is not guilty in the Lord's reck-
oning, the heart that hides no treason. 3 While
I kept my own secret, evermore I went sighing,
so wasted my frame away, 4 bowed down day
and night by thy chastisement; still my strength
ebbed, faint as in mid-summer heat. 5 At last I
made my transgression known to thee, and hid
my sin no longer; Fault of mine, said I, I here
confess to the Lord; and with that, thou didst
remit the guilt of my sin. 6 Let every devout soul,
then, turn to thee in prayer when hard times be-
fall; rise the floods never so high, they shall have
no power to reach it. 7 Thou art my hiding-place,
when I am sore bestead; songs of triumph are
all about me, and thou my deliverer. 8 Friend,

let me counsel thee, trace for thee the path thy
feet should tread; let my prudence watch over
thee. 9 Do not be like the horse and the mule,
senseless creatures which will not come near thee
unless their spirit is tamed by bit and bridle. 10
Again and again the sinner must feel the lash; he
who trusts in the Lord finds nothing but mercy
all around him. 11 Just souls, be glad, and rejoice
in the Lord; true hearts, make your boast in him.

Psalm 37.

2 Domine, ne in furore tuo arguas me,
neque in ira tua corripias me: 3 quoniam sagittæ
tuæ infixæ sunt mihi, et confirmasti super me
manum tuam. 4 Non est sanitas in carne mea,
a facie iræ tuæ; non est pax ossibus meis, a facie peccatorum meorum: 5 quoniam iniquitates
meæ supergressæ sunt caput meum, et sicut
onus grave gravatæ sunt super me. 6 Putruerunt
et corruptæ sunt cicatrices meæ, a facie insipi-

entiæ meæ. 7 Miser factus sum et curvatus sum usque in finem; tota die contristatus ingrediebar. 8 Quoniam lumbi mei impleti sunt illusionibus, et non est sanitas in carne mea. 9 Afflictus sum, et humiliatus sum nimis; rugiebam a gemitu cordis mei. 10 Domine, ante te omne desiderium meum, et gemitus meus a te non est absconditus. 11 Cor meum conturbatum est; dereliquit me virtus mea, et lumen oculorum meorum, et ipsum non est mecum. 12 Amici mei et proximi mei adversum me appropinquaverunt, et steterunt; et qui juxta me erant, de longe steterunt: et vim faciebant qui quærebant animam meam. 13 Et qui inquirebant mala mihi, locuti sunt vanitates, et dolos tota die meditabantur. 14 Ego autem, tamquam surdus, non audiebam; et sicut mutus non aperiens os suum. 15 Et factus sum sicut homo non audiens, et non habens in ore suo redargutiones. 16 Quoniam in te, Domine, speravi; tu exaudies me, Domine Deus meus. 17 Quia dixi: Nequando supergaudeant mihi inimici mei; et dum commoventur pedes mei, super me magna locuti sunt. 18 Quoniam ego in flagella paratus sum, et dolor meus in conspectu meo semper. 19 Quoniam iniquitatem meam annuntiabo, et cogitabo pro peccato meo. 20 Inimici autem mei vivunt, et confirmati sunt super me : et multiplicati sunt qui oderunt me inique. 21 Qui retribuunt mala pro bonis detrahebant mihi, quoniam sequebar bonitatem. 22 Ne derelinquas me, Domine Deus meus ; ne discesseris a me. 23 Intende in adjutorium meum, Domine Deus salutis meæ.

2 Thy reproof, Lord, not thy vengeance ; thy chastisement, not thy condemnation ! 3 Thy arrows pierce me, thy hand presses me hard ; 4 thy anger has driven away all health from my body, never a bone sound in it, so grievous are my sins. 5 My own wrong-doing towers high above me, hangs on me like a heavy burden ; 6 my wounds fester and rankle, with my own folly to blame. 7 Beaten down, bowed to the earth, I go mourning all day long, 8 my whole frame afire, my whole

body diseased; 9 so spent, so crushed, I groan aloud in the weariness of my heart. 10 Thou, Lord, knowest all my longings, no complaint of mine escapes thee; 11 restless my heart, gone my strength; the very light that shone in my eyes is mine no longer. 12 Friends and neighbours that meet me keep their distance from a doomed man; old companions shun me. 13 Ill-wishers that grudge me life itself lay snares about me, threaten me with ruin; relentlessly their malice plots against me. 14 And I, all the while, am deaf to their threats, dumb before my accusers; 15 mine the unheeding ear, and the tongue that utters no defense. 16 On thee, Lord, my hopes are set; thou, O Lord my God, wilt listen to me. 17 Such is the prayer I make. Do not let my enemies triumph over me, boast of my downfall. 18 Fall full well I may; misery clouds my view; 19 I am ever ready to publish my guilt, ever anxious over my sin. 20 Unprovoked, their malice still prevails; so many that bear me a grudge so wantonly, 21 rewarding good with evil, and for the very right-

ness of my cause assailing me. 22 Do not fail me,
O Lord my God, do not forsake me; 23 hasten
to my defense, O Lord, my only refuge.

Psalm 50.

3 Miserere mei, Deus, secundum magnam
misericordiam tuam; et secundum multitudinem
miserationum tuarum, dele iniquitatem meam. 4
Amplius lava me ab iniquitate mea, et a peccato
meo munda me. 5 Quoniam iniquitatem meam
ego cognosco, et peccatum meum contra me est
semper. 6 Tibi soli peccavi, et malum coram te
feci; ut justificeris in sermonibus tuis, et vincas
cum judicaris. 7 Ecce enim in iniquitatibus con-
ceptus sum, et in peccatis concepit me mater mea.
8 Ecce enim veritatem dilexisti; incerta et occulta
sapientiæ tuæ manifestasti mihi. 9 Asperges me
hyssopo, et mundabor; lavabis me, et super niv-
em dealbabor. 10 Auditui meo dabis gaudium et
lætitiam, et exsultabunt ossa humiliata. 11 Averte

faciem tuam a peccatis meis, et omnes iniquitates
meas dele. 12 Cor mundum crea in me, Deus,
et spiritum rectum innova in visceribus meis. 13
Ne projicias me a facie tua, et spiritum sanctum
tuum ne auferas a me. 14 Redde mihi lætitiam
salutaris tui, et spiritu principali confirma me. 15
Docebo iniquos vias tuas, et impii ad te conver-
tentur. 16 Libera me de sanguinibus, Deus, Deus
salutis meæ, et exsultabit lingua mea justitiam
tuam. 17 Domine, labia mea aperies, et os meum
annuntiabit laudem tuam. 18 Quoniam si voluiss-
es sacrificium, dedissem utique; holocaustis non
delectaberis. 19 Sacrificium Deo spiritus con-
tribulatus; cor contritum et humiliatum, Deus,
non despicies. 20 Benigne fac, Domine, in bona
voluntate tua Sion, ut ædificentur muri Jerusalem.
21 Tunc acceptabis sacrificium justitiæ, obla-
tiones et holocausta; tunc imponent super altare
tuum vitulos.

3 Have mercy on me, O God, as thou art
ever rich in mercy; in the abundance of thy com-

passion, blot out the record of my misdeeds. 4 Wash me clean, cleaner yet, from my guilt, purge me of my sin, 5 the guilt which I freely acknowledge, the sin which is never lost to my sight. 6 Thee only my sins have offended; it is thy will I have disobeyed; thy sentence was deserved, and still when thou givest award thou hast right on thy side. 7 For indeed, I was born in sin; guilt was with me already when my mother conceived me. 8 But thou art a lover of faithfulness, and now, deep in my heart, thy wisdom has instructed me. 9 Sprinkle me with a wand of hyssop, and I shall be clean; washed, I shall be whiter than snow; 10 tidings send me of good news and rejoicing, and the body that lies in the dust shall thrill with pride. 11 Turn thy eyes away from my sins, blot out the record of my guilt; 12 my God, bring a clean heart to birth within me; breathe new life, true life, into my being. 13 Do not banish me from thy presence, do not take thy holy spirit away from me; 14 give me back the comfort of thy saving power, and strengthen me in generous resolve. 15 So will I teach the wicked to follow thy paths; sinners shall come back to thy obedience. 16 My God, my divine Deliverer, save me from the guilt of bloodshed! This tongue shall boast of thy mercies; 17 O Lord, thou wilt open my lips, and my mouth shall tell of thy praise. 18 Thou hast no mind for sacrifice, burnt-offerings, if I brought them, thou wouldst refuse; 19 here, O God, is my sacrifice, a broken spirit; a heart that is humbled and contrite thou, O God, wilt never disdain. 20 Lord, in thy great love send prosperity to Sion, so that the walls of Jerusalem may rise again. 21 Then indeed thou wilt take pleasure in solemn sacrifice, in gift and burnt-offering; then indeed bullocks will be laid upon thy altar.

Psalm 101.

2 Domine, exaudi orationem meam, et clamor meus ad te veniat. 3 Non avertas faciem tuam a me: in quacumque die tribulor, inclina ad

me aurem tuam; in quacumque die invocavero te, velociter exaudi me. 4 Quia defecerunt sicut fumus dies mei, et ossa mea sicut cremium aruerunt. 5 Percussus sum ut foenum, et aruit cor meum, quia oblitus sum comedere panem meum. 6 A voce gemitus mei adhaesit os meum carni meæ. 7 Similis factus sum pellicano solitudinis; factus sum sicut nycticorax in domicilio. 8 Vigilavi, et factus sum sicut passer solitarius in tecto. 9 Tota die exprobrabant mihi inimici mei, et qui laudabant me adversum me jurabant: 10 quia cinerem tamquam panem manducabam, et potum meum cum fletu miscebam, 11 a facie iræ et indignationis tuæ: quia elevans allisisti me. 12 Dies mei sicut umbra declinaverunt, et ego sicut foenum arui. 13 Tu autem, Domine, in æternum permanes, et memoriale tuum in generationem et generationem. 14 Tu exsurgens misereberis Sion, quia tempus miserendi ejus, quia venit tempus: 15 quoniam placuerunt servis tuis lapides ejus, et terræ ejus miserebuntur. 16 Et timebunt gentes nomen tuum, Domine, et omnes reges

terræ gloriam tuam: 17 quia ædificavit Dominus
Sion, et videbitur in gloria sua. 18 Respexit in
orationem humilium et non sprevit precem
eorum. 19 Scribantur hæc in generatione altera,
et populus qui creabitur laudabit Dominum. 20
Quia prospexit de excelso sancto suo; Dominus
de cælo in terram aspexit: 21 ut audiret gemitus
compeditorum; ut solveret filios interemptor-
um: 22 ut annuntient in Sion nomen Domini,
et laudem ejus in Jerusalem: 23 in conveniendo
populos in unum, et reges, ut serviant Domino.
24 Respondit ei in via virtutis suæ: Paucitatem
dierum meorum nuntia mihi: 25 ne revoces me
in dimidio dierum meorum, in generationem et
generationem anni tui. 26 Initio tu, Domine, terram fundasti, et opera manuum tuarum sunt cæli.
27 Ipsi peribunt, tu autem permanes; et omnes
sicut vestimentum veterascent. Et sicut opertor-
ium mutabis eos, et mutabuntur; 28 tu autem
idem ipse es, et anni tui non deficient. 29 Filii
servorum tuorum habitabunt, et semen eorum in
sæculum dirigetur.

2 O Lord, hear my prayer, and let my cry come unto thee. 3 Do not turn thy face away from me, but lend me thy ear in time of affliction; give me swift audience whenever I call upon thee. 4 See how this life of mine passes away like smoke, how this frame wastes like a tinder! 5 Drained of strength, like grass the sun scorches, I leave my food untasted, forgotten; 6 I am spent with sighing, till my skin clings to my bones. 7 I am no better than a pelican out in the desert, an owl on some ruined dwelling; 8 I keep mournful watch, lonely as a single sparrow on the house top. 9 Still my enemies taunt me, in their mad rage make a by-word of me. 10 Ashes are all my food, I drink nothing but what comes to me mingled with my tears; 11 I shrink before thy vengeful anger, so low thou hast brought me, who didst once lift me so high. 12 Like a tapering shadow my days dwindle, wasting away, like grass in the sun! 13 Lord, thou endurest forever, thy name, age after age, is not forgotten; 14 surely thou wilt bestir thyself, and give Sion redress! It is time, now, to

take pity on her, the hour has come. 15 See how thy servants love her even in ruin, how they water her dust with their tears! 16 Will not the heathen learn reverence, Lord, for thy glorious name, all those monarchs of the earth, 17 when they hear that the Lord has built Sion anew; that he has revealed himself there in glory, 18 has given heed to the prayer of the afflicted, neglects their appeal no more? 19 Such legend inscribe we for a later age to read it; a new people will arise, to praise the Lord; 20 the Lord, who looks down from his sanctuary on high, viewing earth from heaven, 21 who has listened to the groans of the prisoners, delivered a race that was doomed to die. 22 There will be talk of the Lord's name in Sion, of his praise in Jerusalem, 23 when peoples and kings meet there to pay him their homage. 24 Here, on my journey, he has brought my strength to an end, cut short my days. 25 What, my God, wilt thou snatch me away, my life half done? Age after age thy years endure; 26 it was thou, Lord, that didst lay the foundations of earth when time began, it was thy hand that built the heavens. 27 They will perish, but thou wilt remain; they will all be like a cloak that grows threadbare, and thou wilt lay them aside like a garment, and exchange them for new; 28 thou art unchanging, thy years can never fail. 29 The posterity of thy servants shall yet hold their lands in peace, their race shall live on in thy keeping.

Psalm 125.

1 De profundis clamavi ad te, Domine; 2 Domine, exaudi vocem meam. Fiant aures tuæ intendentes in vocem deprecationis meæ. 3 Si iniquitates observaveris, Domine, Domine, quis sustinebit? 4 Quia apud te propitiatio est; et propter legem tuam sustinui te, Domine. Sustinuit anima mea in verbo ejus: 5 speravit anima mea in Domino. 6 A custodia matutina usque ad noctem, speret Israel in Domino. 7 Quia apud Dominum misericordia, et copiosa apud eum redemptio. 8 Et ipse redimet Israel ex omnibus iniquitatibus ejus.

1 Out of the depths have I cried unto Thee, O Lord; 2 Lord, hear my voice! Let Thine ears be attentive to the voice of my supplications. 3 If Thou, Lord, shouldest mark iniquities, O Lord, who shall stand? 4 But there is forgiveness with Thee, that Thou mayest be feared. 5 I wait for the Lord, my soul doth wait, and in His word do I hope. 6 My soul waiteth for the Lord more than they that watch for the morning— I say, more than they that watch for the morning. 7 Let Israel hope in the Lord, for with the Lord there is mercy, and with Him is plenteous redemption. 8 And He shall redeem Israel from all his iniquities.

Psalm 142.

1 Domine, exaudi orationem meam; auribus percipe obsecrationem meam in veritate tua; exaudi me in tua justitia. 2 Et non intres in judicium cum servo tuo, quia non justificabitur in conspectu tuo omnis vivens. 3 Quia perse-

cutus est inimicus animam meam; humiliavit in terra vitam meam; collocavit me in obscuris, sicut mortuos sæculi. 4 Et anxiatus est super me spiritus meus; in me turbatum est cor meum. 5 Memor fui dierum antiquorum; meditatus sum in omnibus operibus tuis: in factis manuum tuarum meditabar. 6 Expandi manus meas ad te; anima mea sicut terra sine aqua tibi. 7 Velociter exaudi me, Domine; defecit spiritus meus. Non avertas faciem tuam a me, et similis ero descendentibus in lacum. 8 Auditam fac mihi mane misericordiam tuam, quia in te speravi. Notam fac mihi viam in qua ambulem, quia ad te levavi animam meam. 9 Eripe me de inimicis meis, Domine: ad te confugi. 10 Doce me facere voluntatem tuam, quia Deus meus es tu. Spiritus tuus bonus deducet me in terram rectam. 11 Propter nomen tuum, Domine, vivificabis me: in æquitate tua, educes de tribulatione animam meam, 12 et in misericordia tua disperdes inimicos meos, et perdes omnes qui tribulant animam meam, quoniam ego servus tuus sum.

1 Listen, Lord, to my prayer; give my plea a hearing, as thou art ever faithful; listen, thou who lovest the right. 2 Do not call thy servant to account; what man is there living that can stand guiltless in thy presence? 3 See how my enemies plot against my life, how they have abased me in the dust, set me down in dark places, like the long-forgotten dead! 4 My spirits are crushed within me, my heart is cowed. 5 And my mind goes back to past days; I think of all thou didst once, dwell on the proofs thou gavest of thy power. 6 To thee I spread out my hands in prayer, for thee my soul thirsts, like a land parched with drought. 7 Hasten, Lord, to answer my prayer; my spirit grows faint. Do not turn thy face away from me, and leave me like one sunk in the abyss. 8 Speedily let me win thy mercy, my hope is in thee; to thee I lift up my heart, shew me the path I must follow; 9 to thee I fly for refuge, deliver me, Lord, from my enemies. 10 Thou art my God, teach me to do thy will; let thy gracious spirit lead me, safe ground under my

feet. 11 For the honour of thy own name, Lord, grant me life; in thy mercy rescue me from my cruel affliction. 12 Have pity on me, and scatter my enemies; thy servant I; make an end of my cruel persecutors.

END OF SUPPLEMENT.